# Poems in PERSPEX

Max Harris Poetry Award 2007

Max Harris Poetry Award 2007

Edited by
Ioana Petrescu
Cameron Fuller
Gill Ratcliff

LYTHRUM PRESS 2008
in association with the
Poetry and Poetics Centre, UniSA

First published by
Lythrum Press
PO Box 243 Rundle Mall
Adelaide SA

October 2008

in association with the
Poetry and Poetics Centre
University of South Australia
St Bernards Road
Magill SA 5072
http://poetryandpoeticscentre.com
Director: Dr Ioana Petrescu



ISBN 978 1 921013 23 2

Cover image: Megan Boyd who dedicates the cover to Anne Ogg
Designed and typeset by Michael Deves, Lythrum Press
Printed and bound by Griffin Digital

# Contents

# Foreword

## Samela Harris

Anthologies have a particular beauty in the way in which they collect and distil creative juices.

They have a fairness of exposure, an equality of individuality and a satisfaction of reading—or so it has seemed to me for these many years since *The Penguin Book of Australian Verse*, edited by John Thompson, was on the school curriculum.

To me it was the most enriching and endlessly distracting book containing a wonder world of styles and metres, thoughts and images—as well as a timeline of the country's literary evolution, ideas, mores and cultural iconography.

Max Harris was in there, of course, with his best-known lyric and narrative poems taking their place in the country's poetic landscape.

Mine was the privilege not only of knowing the poet but of witnessing his creative processes and, sometimes, the violence of the muse which could cut abruptly into family life and drag him off to pen and paper behind a closed door.

For Max, even from the raw childhood years in which he began his prodigious poetic output, poetic composition was a private process. Feisty newspaper columns he could, and did, handwrite amid a human hubbub in a pub or restaurant, but poetry always took him away to dark corners.

My fortune as the poet's child was the getting to know a lot of the poets I admired and, vicariously, to enjoy the fellowship among writers.

Of course, they were as diverse as their works—and they walked many paths in life, for poetry rarely becomes a living.

Max supported his family in the bookshop and journalism business. For him, every aspect of life was always all about the words, articulation, communication, ideas ... the intellectual processes, the fruit of thought.

What set him apart from other poets was what we would now call his outreach. He was a man of rare intellectual and creative generosity. If a young poet asked for guidance, it would come accompanied by encouragement and genuine interest, a powerful wish to see others do well, especially if it promised to add something to the pool of higher sensibilities. This was a cause Max espoused—the stretching of the wings of thought. Many were the hopefuls who came to Max and were read, considered and steered. Many.

One wondered at this generosity of spirit and energy. Like creative writing, it seemed borne of a compulsion—and, perhaps, a need to give what was never given to him. Max suffered a father who viewed poetry with contempt and, of course, the brave new modernism of his callow youth was to embroil him in literary controversy which was never quite to go away. Ern Malley lives. And so does the indomitable and altruistic spirit of Max Harris.

Thus does the Max Harris Poetry Award mirror the quintessence of Max Harris, both man and poet. This ensuing anthology not only airs the work of a very fine array of contemporary poets but also it reflects the discernment of its editors. Their role is to bring cohesion to the allsorts of individuality and give us this pleasure of a publication through which we can pick and pause and ponder. While we may read it in whichever order takes our fancy, one becomes very conscious of the fact that this book has a very special place on the map of Australian cultural iconography.

# Poetry

## Winner of the Max Harris Poetry Award 2007

Jan Owen

### Scent, Comb, Spoon

Even the might-have-been returns.
The simplest thing—scent, comb, spoon—
and it sweeps back streaming bright dust toward the sun,
an abandoned chaos that needs to be known,
an insistence thirsty for history, hungry for soul.
He writes the idea down,

recalling how they watched two otters once—
that sinuous skein more fluid than water itself.
Do thought and feeling twine like that,
a spiral helix speeding time?
Now the water has stilled to calm
reflection and disappearance keep faith.

But where does it go to, really, he wonders,
or come back from?
Is this what resurrection means,
a flicker of cells, a taste for symmetry?
Drop a dimension, and what was it all about?
His irony's nervous tic is a grey shortcut:

***"Give me a steady hand, a watchful eye, that none may suffer hurt when I pass by.***
***Thou givest life; I pray no act of mine may take away or mar that gift of Thine.***
***Shield those, dear Lord, who bear me company from foolish folk and all calamity.***
***Teach me to use my car for others' need, let me not miss, through witless love of speed,***
***The beauties of Thy world, that thus I may with joy and courtesy go on my way."***

**CAR BOGGED: If you are bogged and you are near a saw mill, sawdust will get your car out quickly.**

## Car in Garage

Prevent it from hitting the wall by suspending an old tyre from the ceiling on a rope ; position it in front of car's bumper.

*"I have suffered many things in this life, most of which has never happened."*

## Carpet (small article lost)

To find a small object dropped on the carpet, pull a stocking over the vacuum cleaner hose, fasten securely and sweep over the area. The cleaner will suck the object into the stocking.

## Chair Painting

Put foil under legs, instead of newspaper. Paint does not stick to foil.

*"He who watches the clock will always remain one of the hands."*

## Clock Ticks Drowned

Place large glass bowl over clock then you can still see the time, hear alarm, but won't hear the tick or, place a piece of spongy foam under it.

## Contact Lens

If you drop one, make the room dark, then shine a torch over the floor and the lens will sparkle in the light.

two hesitations *er er*
in a declaration of love,
the question-answer in a mock debate,
or less, the single apostrophes either end
of an anecdote with a lame punchline—
'two dark wings that could not lift our bird to flight'.
And the joint citation for commonsense,
was it conscience, confusion, or cowardice?
*Music vanishes into itself*, he writes,
*Words swim back through words*, things of that sort.
He's reading a book on Scythia bought for a song.
They say she's taken up golf.

What's left? A taste for blue.
And a keepsake to outlast them both—
the mid-month moon lugging its unseen half
like cherished flesh. There is a wholeness
to almost everything.

# Highly commended

## sarah k bell

### the crows

the proper term for a crowd of crows
is murder        the blackest of deaths

    tatty reapers with great hacking coughs splitting

the air thick & tasting of
    fingerprints     salt
    in the earth     in a vase
                     whose flowers have long since been spread over the estate

*

having spent all our money we prepare for death
checking each of our pieces for wear & clucking
hoarse           rattling
our voices       the spare keys

take me driving
i want to hear this rusty shell
    split        like a new egg        which does not
    crack                    but instead
    tear
                                       divides smoothly

flimsy filmy skin
interrupted by bone

its centre          pale &
still          no chirping of life

*

& the crows come in to land
from surrounding cities

a massacre

# Katerina Kokkinos-Kennedy

## Farewell

With an ostentatious disregard for usual practices,
We took you home and settled you into the kitchen.
The tactless faux-hardwood poly-satin lined coffin
Winded us with its total assault on good taste.

Cooking bacon and eggs we played at normality and
Your uncharacteristic silence made cowards of us
Twitching now and then in the periphery you threatened,
Like Frankenstein, to jolt back into being.

Unnerved by imaginings and wild late winter winds
We took to sentry guard two at a time to keep watch
Our Poe-like paranoia quietly adding terrors to the night
In which a raven would have been no oddity.

Time-suspended, we rode for days through the strangest
Of landscapes where little moved and less breathed
Surrounded by unmoving water, stone and stillness
We learned how hard it is to spend time with the dead.

The half-hearted roasts were devoured in obdurate silence
In defiance of your uncompromisingly writ large state;
We ate to say, 'I am alive and this, this thing here—is not I'
You became our kitchen pharaoh, ruling us even now.

On the last night we grew reckless and loud-mouthed
Like pagans fuelled by too much grog and gnawing fear
Stories shot from our raucous and loosened mouths
And as one eye cried—the other roared with laughter.

It was a fine sending off but after the burial when we returned
To the emptied house, exhausted by speeches, tears and the
Grasping arms of loving strangers, we were sated and collapsed
Gratefully weeping on the narrow survivors' couch.

## Commended

## Joan Kerr

### Captain Foster Fyans

(This poem is based on the account of Captain Fyans
given in Robert Hughes' *The Fatal Shore*, 1987.)

I picked you out, among these local worthies,
              grave sirs, as respectable
as mutton-chop whiskers can make them, framed

              in municipal oak.
You have a bold, bland stare in a face like a brick
              good, plain, commonsense

brick, sir, and I call a ruffian a ruffian.
              By God, we had some sport
with them, the cats unravelling for the work

              (and the floggers not much better,
complaining of the heat and wanting beer)
              and still the villains

faced it out in silence. Stone men, they called themselves.
              Stone men! Well I
can make stones sing, I can make stones long for death,

              and yet refuse it.
Out here, the titled ones, colonels and such
              fall by the wayside soon enough.

Good plain honest soldiers rule the roost
                and a man can rise,
as I have, as you see. Magistrate, city founder

                owner of acres
and a stately residence, that gives a man respect,
                gives him a lasting name.

*

Hard to believe, in our touchy-feely age,
                it didn't do some damage
that you didn't wake, perhaps in winter nights

                when frost was delivering
the trees from pleasant muffling, that you didn't think
                how, showing off, you used

the metaphor of frost for what the cat-
                o'-nine-tails did to flesh,
how you drew out the metaphor, from frost the first stroke,

                snow the next and then the third
*why then the blood flows freely.* How you proposed
                *to flog a fellow for you*

*so you may observe.* Hard to believe you didn't
                sometimes turn, dressing, and look
over your shoulder at the solid flesh sitting

                easy on the bones. Then stretch out
both your arms and hold the mirror giving back
                yourself, the magistrate

framed in mahogany. Ordered sounds of the house,
                outside, as far as the river
your peaceful lawns, still faintly traced with frost.

# Mark Miller

## Postcards from the Coast

**1 Winter Beach, Morning**

A crescent moon,
the beach and tea-trees
are bleakest at dawn

with crows picking at weed
and sea-wrack on the steely sand.

Above the thrum
of returning boats
voices toss on the spume

first boardriders of winter
slice through the water

and beyond the sandbar the sun,
squeezed up from the horizon,
is cut loose
and stains the sea in blood.

**2 Estuary at Low Tide**

At low tide the wind's finger
crinkles the gulls
volplaning over the estuary—

on the edge of the curving shoreline
three fishermen
stand as still as boulders

a lone jogger's shirt
is a tiny stab of red
in the cool opalescence of air.

**3 Afternoon, Beneath a Sun-Tight Sky**

Startled,
a flurry of terns
unstitches the hem,
trails silver threads
from the estuary's
fine lace-edge.

*

Tattooed in shade
of marram grasses,
a white-faced heron
stands in frozen silence.

*

Darting minnows,
a fistful of pebbles,
stipple the shallows.

*

Along the shore
shadows of the pines
are a thick black calligraphy.

*

Overhead,
a necklace of gulls
rattles the empty bowl of sky.

**4 Moon Over the Estuary**

After the dusk's slow
inhalation of light

the reticent moon appears
from behind the trees.

Soundlessly, she climbs
the blank staircase of sky

her sequined gown trailing
over the black skin of the estuary.

See how she moves
like mercury through the water

the stars her unstringed pearls
spilling on the floor of the world.

## Jude Aquilina

### Three small lives

**Moth *Agrotis infusa***
I am the plain, hairy cousin
of that graceful, gaudy show-off.
I'm out on the town, while she's
fast asleep. I stop at the first
lit window, soliciting other night-life.
I fling myself at the seamy element:
anything hot and white.
The moon is a sleazy pimp
spurning this orgy under a public lamp.
I whirl in frenzied circles with the mob,
my dress a torn mess,
I'm dizzy and drunk on light.

**Rhinoceros Beetle *Xylotrupes Ulysses***
All horn and armour
a black knight ready to joust
but slowed down by heavy mail
and clunky breastplates.
By the time he makes the arena
the princess is a crone
and he's overturned
by an army of ants.

**Cricket *Acheta domesticus***

The cricket is a monk in the order *insecta*,
chanting sweet plainsong into the night,
taking my mind to other planes that vibrate
with memories, all linked by the smell
of gum leaves and summer rain.

## Peter Bakowski

### At 10 Rosebank Terrace, Lower Templestowe

Fights between our father and mother in the family kitchen,
after returning from another party,
where our father had again flirted, danced close with other women,
ignored our mother for most of the evening.

Fights where plates were thrown and smashed,
the worst swear words in Polish and German were shouted, spat.
Fights with the sounds
of our mother being hit, slapped across the face,
our father storming out of the house,
driving away in the family car,
our mother sweeping together the broken pieces of crockery
scattered across the kitchen floor.

After such fights our mother grew silent.
She'd go a whole day, two days, three days,
without speaking one word to any of us.
Beds were made,
washing was hung,
meals were served.
Morning became midnight then dawn
in our waiting house.

'Another piece of toast?'
'You need new shoelaces.'
The silence was broken,
but the divorce came.
In the settlement our mother got the house.

Now on Sundays
my brother and I visit her there.
We play cards.
There's talk about
the weather, the price of fruit and vegetables,
grouchy Mr Collings next door,
whose wife is never seen.

There's lunch,
toasted rolls with slices of cheese, ham, salami,
cups of filtered coffee,
biscuits and chocolates.

Our mother tells us
she's thankful for what she's got,
doesn't go to church,
but sometimes when gardening,
looks up at the sky, asks God
to let her die in her sleep,
like uncle Gerhard.

My brother and I assure her
that she'll live to past ninety
like her father.

Lunch finished
we rise from our places
at the kitchen table,
our offers to help
clear the table, wash the dishes,
refused again.

# Elaine Barker

## Frederick Franklin's Photograph

The photographer has positioned the hunting party
clustered around their Chrysler
and in front of a tidy limestone house.
The men are well equipped against the cold
with hats and boots and overcoats.
Suits are crumpled and second best
yet good enough for a hunting trip.
There's a claim to training and expertise
in the precise slope of their rifles;
in South Africa perhaps, against the Boer.
Gold watch chains dangle grandly
across the surfeit of each portly chest.
The image's reverse carries the photographer's stamp
and faded names in copperplate: Henry and Edward,
Leonard and Albert, Harold and Jack.
You can catch the jokes, the colour of their laughter,
the facile songs and the drinking after.

In the background, there's a cottage garden
with a gravel path and a picket fence
and much further on,
paddocks flagged with unruly gums.
Here was the hunting ground of men
who finding themselves in focus
slipped away beyond this frame.
They timed the seasons and marked the skies,
passed lightly over these sepia plains.

# David Best

## returning

the dawn
bleeds the light, dropping the day

which breathes
into being with birdsong and the

sizzle song
of insects persistent as the sun

the world
smells warm, leafmould wet, lustful;

life stretches
saying nothing, only smiling

the soul awake
–i've been here before, dimly:

remembering is
hard–the accent was different then

colours less
in your face, the air grey and muted,

the sky
less endless and a certain settled blue

this land
is something else again, though we tart it up

and mutter:
be hidden; let me alone for as long as you can

## Belinda Broughton

### What Wind Is

You think of wind
as storms in pines
or willy-willies on hot earth,
tornadoes or cyclones,
or snatching at your hat
or flipping your umbrella inside out.
You think of wind
as marks on weather maps,
arrows around the globe.
You think of wind
as a great big thing
inevitable off the sea,
rushing in to fill the space
where warmth rises from the land.

But ...
think of it ...
it is the little gasp
drawn through your teeth
or mouthed around her name
or whispered onto her nipple.

# Gerard Butera

## My Higher Self

This is my stop coming up, just as I finish my novel.
My Higher Self has timed it this way.

It also has me turn on the radio or TV as the presenter is saying,
*For those who have just tuned in ...*

I never miss a thing.

The tram doors part to present the world.
Orange. Pink. Edgeless.

First out is The Power Dresser.
We only ever nod. It would be too much to discuss the sunset as auteur.

The breeze is from the north,
the temperature of a tape left on a dashboard.

In the park, three bikes sleep under a tree.

I untuck my shirt,
undo some buttons.

There's That Guy Who's Always Skulking Around.
He's passing a note to The Wind Chime Woman

*thanks for not hating me because I spit on your footpath because I have three front teeth missing because I notice your open windows*

She continues watering her sage plants,
thinking about his *E*s.
How they are all back-to-front.

Her feeling about him
right all along.

As usual, The Old Woman At Number 40
sits staring out her front window.
Counting the hours on her rosary beads.

I have fallen in love with the young woman she was
before she left the hills of Calabria.

Gathering up her hand-made dress
to carry the figs.
She would look, and look away,
when young men came to buy a goat from her father.

Tonight she waves. But I am not the angel who will
take her back to *il paese vecchio.*

All—most—home, I say,
landing each footstep heavy
on a syllable,
thinking of my couch—my TV—my dinner
when the cicada choir holds its breath.

Only now do I hear it.

## David Campbell

### Redemption

She lifts her hands to pray, kneels
beside my bed, head bowed, eyes
closed in a denial of reality; traps
the truth in steepled fingers that

barely touch, for to do so recalls
his hands on my skin, night-breath
in my hair, bruising the darkness
with muffled cries. *Oh ... oh ... oh*

*Lord, Almighty Father* ... her voice
stumbles for she knows, but only
in some place buried deep, deep
down beneath the daily routine,

polishing the purity of her mind
with the whipped cream civility
of her kind. *Forgive us our sins* ...
especially his, for she will not

confront him, but turns her eyes
instead towards heaven, seeking
in her faith to summon some relief
from horror. She distracts herself

each evening with needlepoint, head
bowed over the welcome pattern
of two dimensional life; thrusts
her guilt precisely into the fabric,

blending bright contrasting textures
as she weaves a piano, a delicate
vase of flowers, an old log cabin
with a rocking chair on a veranda

in a meadow with gum trees. Her
world becomes the fluting call
of the magpie and the sharp tang
of woodsmoke on a crisp morning

when the track of a fox pockmarks
the ice-frosted grass. She conjures
visions of a family at peace singing
sweetly in harmony ... *and forgive*

*those who sin against us. Lead us*
*not into temptation* ... her hand rises
and falls, floss strands perfectly flat.
Her work is meticulous, the needle

hanging free to straighten the twists
in her dream, the unspoken thought
that can never be undone. Intricate
palette stitches enhance the design.

*Deliver us from evil* ... she prays for
my soul. It is my fault the door opens
on innocence in the still, dead hours
before dawn when smothered cries

are lost in feigned sleep. *For thine*
*is the kingdom* ... she weeps for my
childhood, carefully unpicks each
thread of my life for her own rich

tapestry of shame. That is her only
redemption ... *the power and the glory*
*for ever and ever ... please forgive me,*
*Lord, and absolve all my sins. Amen.*

# Gaylene Carbis

## The Kalimna

here i am with my fond memories of the Kalimna
now gone replaced by five hundred thousand dollar apartments.
you are one of those people who have a favourite place in the world aside from Paris:
the Great Ocean Road leading to Lorne and the Kalimna waiting at the end of it
like a great goddess looking down on her people in the valley below.
there it waited for our beginning. here i am in the first place you bring me
to show me your world and draw me into it. there is our courtship at some stage ashes.
the bulldozers came and pulled it down and we stood and watched the dirt as if
it would rise up and bring back the Kalimna. there is our courtship
replaced by five hundred thousand dollar apartments.

here i am in the Kalimna and this is my first time here these hours are ours.
this is the way you begin to build a life together the places you travel to
the places you leave the ground we gain and the ground we lose.
here you wrote a poem for your forty-seventh birthday
where i am looking out the window before the day even wakes.
there i wrote looking out the window while
you were a poem lying so still as if you were sleeping.
here in the Kalimna where our lovemaking made dates
and anniversaries we failed to keep.
i never wrote about being there i had nothing to say.
i was writing only longing and loss
never here at the Kalimna where i thought i was happy.
you always wrote about love wherever you were.

i discover you honeymooned here your first wife seems surprised
i never knew. so much so much i didn't know.
you brought her here and so many others it's hard not to see you

here at the Kalimna like an aging James Bond living out
fifteen year old fantasies and wet dreams of love.
you open car doors for beautiful women and lovely girls who
are all-legs and always laughing in fancy hotel rooms.
i wonder as you sign in if the Manager is discreet
doesn't look out to see who you're with this time
sees only the shadows of women floating past
wet from the water like sirens rising from the sea.
your holiday destinations are like listening to the same song
over and over just sung by a few different singers who give
the semblance of difference.

here at home you've planned another trip to Lorne
the Kalimna's gone now. how we miss those special places
that take us back to that particular time and place
and a face we remember. here at home i mention the Kalimna
and you speak to me as if i'm a stranger: '*Did you ever go there?*'
and there i am with my memories meaning nothing if i ever
stayed at the Kalimna i was alone and never knew i was lonely.

all the lovers you've ever had tell me you've talked for twenty years
of living in Lorne the poetry you'll write in the house by the sea
the house you'd build for poetry to live
a house in the country! a house in the city!
and the *life*, oh the *Life* you'd give them!

all of us.

now gone.

## Kim Core

### The Connoisseur

*for Rosemary Dobson*

I could never understand
a wine connoisseur
the way he took a whiff
a mouthful
swirled it round
had a think
then spat it out

put into context
a good poem in a good year
is in the tasting

I try and place her
the fragrance of remembrance
a continuance of Brueghels
a foundation of Matisse
it's the expressiveness of colour
No.  It's the depth
if one could speak of a quality
Malaga—a Picasso
No—a Van Gogh
But, yes, a Picasso but not Malaga
a Gauguin a Cezanne
kissed by the wind
I feel a more hearty red
with smidges of green and gold
heralding the exhibition of '39

eclipsed by the moon
Boy, what a year '44
more of a century
holding her own

I hear shades of Longfellow
in this psalm of life
the quality
outlasts
the acidity of the academe
the fickleness in fashion.

## John de Laine

### The Creek

The creek is pre-morning tea, at 9.01,
a coffee machine.
The creek is Sunday, and the end
of the financial year.
The creek is a cigarette, a personal phone
call, Friday, a thank-you note.
The creek is a staff meeting, the boss on a call, a chair that doesn't wobble, a
doughnut, a doughnut,
an eight, in the football tips.
The creek is no deadline,
an open cheque. The creek is denial
of staff cuts, and no cuts.
The creek is a sickie, the creek
is a beach, in winter; the creek is you, the creek
is me. We sit and watch
as copies of Hansard
float past. The creek is a bird,
who sings for no money.
The creek is a car, with its engine off,
its doof-doof down, its driver in contemplation
of life in the days before the wheel.
The creek is a horse drinking,
on the pastoralist's time, and dawdling off
to prance around with the butterflies
that God forgot.
The creek is shoes off,
day off, blood and bone and laughter and new love.
A fistful of grass, the miracle of a pebble,
trout racing by–
sunlight turning their scales to gold
as it peeps through a gap in the skyscrapers.

## jim dodd

### spruikin'

upon a once    fallow    foreign    billion here

billion there    sooner or later    talkin' real money

well    g'day

acceptable compass of perfect sat

four two nine wick

mccracken

spruiken

narrow    visage    segue du jour

wrought stock talk later

little local skin    can

sit bare

on

large ice

no no answer unforthcoming    dipperyslip apple lie vocal

late in a day    e-mail hope bracket prevaricate bracket    ketch thought ride slow

minim    phlegmatic

refract quaver

cheapishuseofavailablelettergroupings remember applicable trajectories

inbound nerve damage hock night life finagle security clear love

a moray call

oe'r sand

dip little mission dip

lo slow woe slick state detail death note holders value return while minimizing
available package damage

lean back enjoy comfy chair love slipper picker smoke
stock checker tape

maintenance plumbers occasionally mistale chop live wires die

woeshow continue featuring

there'd be culture 'n' there'd be civilization

recent struck differential feature

bishop harrop

turbo pump of rocket scientists continue act

quick weather look await soft pattern ties

smiles pack hunt meet australian standard inured principle love moment
senior client advisors not so sure

gambled air little barrier to slow blade thin lip gang manipulate near every

premonition weather

dream

almost love flow

wayward thought host any hat concrete lean easy trickable finger see
grade at grade

another soon

soon

available fate

attend as guest

## Robby Drake

### He sleeps

You snuggle into my breast and smile
play the push and giggle game
against my skin and laugh
with your mouth full

I chat quietly and hope
for a few moments to catch my breath
before you call again
full of energy

Your eyes start to close
and your feet stop pushing
as you relax into the rhythm
suck and swallow

I have to put my finger
gently between your lips
and prize your teeth away
before you feel cheated

You roll slightly away
then snuggle back into my arm
still and relaxed
breathing softly

I stand and carry you
holding you close
place you into your cot
as I kiss your sleeping face.

# Daniel East

## The Rose-seller

The young prince is his own gesture
    an eloquent stride as though
he steps between sedans as might
    some idle giant strolling
between islands  –  his face is
    hidden by a peacock's plume of roses
purse-red close-lipped roses
    belled like women's hips

and behind that ? why –
    nothing there but stems and blossoms.
His smile is the jack of diamonds
    his suit a flute of champagne
fedora cocked atop his grin
    a gold coin tucked into the brim.
He is the Rose-seller  –
    forgetful men remember riding

two hours in forgetful heat
    to rendezvous with red-haired sweethearts
                – and red-haired sweethearts
    picking at salmon crepes
think of greasy sunscreen and salty kisses
    tumblers of soft drink and summer.
No one may buy flowers from the Rose-seller
    for they are fixed like a lock or a lapel

and their skin is his skin and their scent
    his suggestion lingering
in the hearts and loins of thin-lipped old men
    secreting his roses from wet beds of earth
where he lay          –
    though beneath lover's benches
he watches other roses grow
    green-lined from the lawn they perch above

A blue rose shatters from the blonde eye
    of the girl with glossy skin
a crown of bloom from brow to cheek
                          –      showers of roses
tumble flesh-hued from bare shoulders
    or rip from leather and fall black-stitched
from footballs kicked across the court
    men with heavy shoulders tailing

Over here ! A driver who stomps her brakes
    and shouts      –        she too
a chrome rose shyly stretching from the grille
    a bead of oil slipping slow
                          –        Why from all this asphalt street
gravel lifts, blooms and sways like a veil
but the pale air is smudged crystal cut
    a blossom of flame sinking to earth below.

# Carolyn Fisher

## Words on the Wind

Mackerel-net skies are hauled up
from the east emptying a catch of clear horizon
that darkens as the heavy machinery
of thunderheads roll in.
Like a baby's toy hung over a pram
a fuchsia flower bounces on its stem,
stamens strike as if to sound
a gentle tintinnabulation
in a breeze that signifies at least a four
on the Beaufort scale. Yesterday saw
the kind of zero puff that allows a single leaf
to widdershins a plumb line to earth.
Then the escalation: a transition from one number
to the next noted by those adept at sizing up
a breeze and its effect, who study gusts
and the lob and spill of wind-socks
to calculate a rush of air in knots.
A hundred thousand metronomes
in a poppy paddock time a steady rise
until the plum pudding heads bow,
as if to a deity. A five blows to six.
Leaves on the road dance death throes
like small victims of wheels. At seven,
tumble weed of plastic bags roll
straight out of a Western and the wind really
shows its hand, a branch slams to the ground
with the force of a winning card.
This air has roamed the troposphere

and returned with international flavours:
the sound of a Scottish waterfall pours
through the sieve of a gum; the lower half
of the tree turns suddenly to a shoal
of Mediterranean silver-backed sea bream
while upper branches shake their pom-poms
like cheerleaders. Waves hoist a full-rig
against the horizon. On the beach
low-flying sand stings the ankles of windsurfers
heading out for circus tricks on the backs
of a wild white herd. Seagulls head inland.
At high tide mark someone's blown the head
off a hundred pints of beer.
The puppy of a breeze
that chased the tail on a pile of leaves
this morning has blown into a dog of a wind,
straining the leash on every
blade of grass. Not a ten, but at least
an eight and a half ransacks the garden,
shakes small birds loose from bushes,
whistles under the eaves like possums fighting,
halts clear thinking, makes you wonder ...
The storm that scorches Jupiter
rips clouds into coloured ribbons
with its speed, raging over three hundred years.
Can the same words be heard
in the endless bluster
from that hurricane's red mouth
as down the draught of a sea-squall's throat,
or in a westerly's oration: clues
about transience and the constant pressure
that saves you from falling

# Dominique Hecq

## Gifts of the Olive Grove

Dust depends on the leaves of the olive trees
to give it substance. No sound. No sound
but the hiss of the drying grass and flies
whose crystalline eyes shatter the world

into brilliant repetitions. I stand
here often, fabricating delicate lies
that repeat the green to gold to sere
turn of the earth, syllables in a whorl

of light. They dissemble, court, preen
and press against one another, each
giving weight and form to the others'
bodies. Drops of sweat, small pearls,

hang from the branches. The greys and greens
weave their own web: lashes for my eyes.

## Judy Johnson

### Noli Me Tangere

*After Titian's painting, 1515*

This is the first modern landscape,

the scene, not just a backdrop
for the characters who inhabit it, but alight

and incandescent, ignited in the transparency
                                        of the sky's glass skull.

The man is almost to the bottom of the mountain,
the afternoon around him the colour of nectar

that bees have drunk
                                        from molten-copper flowers.

He is poised between steps as though
to reckon the passing hours

by the shadow of the looming house
on the hill behind him,
                                        its many rooms,

the horse-hair brush of sprawling day
currying the flanks of its sloping roof.

Here is Divinity:
            the voluptuous nourishment

of softly folded hills, appearing
          like egg-yolk brioche from the oven,
                              steaming, broken open.

It is God taken down
from the pallid

austere office of his pedestal,
                              transfused

with the rich blood of a flawed and falling world.

What to make of the young Christ
in the foreground?

Holding a sickle above the kneeling girl as though
to reap the fine seeds of her devotion,

set them adrift on a breeze to pollinate clear light.

X rays have shown that Titian painted
another Jesus under this one,

and perhaps another under that.
Each of them in a slightly different pose,

as if the artist could not let
this one particular of the story

go into the void and bounty of everything,
                                        untranslated.

As though he felt, growing old himself, he could finally
leave the over-arching plot of the father alone,

but must instead adjust the masks and costumes
of the son, this one last time,
unravelling the smaller narrative.

Painting over the shame that,
in men who have lived long enough,

is nothing more than the aggregate of loss on loss.

His heart alight under his fingers: cracking,
remaking the specific thing most loved,
most ruined,

until the landscape resolves beyond the canvas:

the fruit still ripe for the picking,
on the still-growing tree
in Adam's garden.

No one, as yet, having mentioned
that a cross is made of timber.

No one gone to fetch the axe.

## Alana Kelsall

### The holes we breathe through

Inching along the barbed wire of birth
her fingers touch the crown
ripping the last thread from the edge
words fold in half

her fingers touch the crown
she slumps in the pockets of houses
words fold in half
trying to pin love down

she slumps in the pockets of houses
phone to her ear
trying to pin love down
when the car pulls out

phone to her ear
she's pruning each fall from grace
when the car pulls out
the sky clamours with windows

she's pruning each fall from grace
the curtains shrink at the slightest breeze
the sky clamours with windows
the next breath in doubt

the curtains shrink at the slightest breeze
trust finds its own shape
the next breath in doubt
no signpost    no flag above the line

trust finds its own shape
boats elbowing their way out
no signpost    no flag above the line
she criss-crosses the wake of her past

boats elbowing their way out
a passage roped to the sea
she criss-crosses the wake of her past
the holes we breathe through

a passage roped to the sea
ripping the last thread from the edge
the holes we breathe through
inching along the barbed wire of birth

# Jeri Kroll

## Swan Dancing

There they are, the old couple,
floating on the seemingly smooth,
he with a foot folded up on his back,
catching the last of the sun,
she snoozing, head under a wing.

Time for a snack? He prods her awake.
As one, they change direction for the reeds,
then mince ashore to forage.
No competition here. This patch is theirs—
and their young's—if they bother to breed.

Mated for life, did she ever regret her choice?
Find he was better at gliding than providing?
When he lost himself in her ruff
she had such downy dreams she never asked
if he'd warm the clutch or mind the cygnets.

No doubts ruffled her feathers that first summer.
He was grand, her lusty courtier,
with plumes to equal the clouds,
a neck, sensuous as sunbeams,
a beak, the colour of harvest moons.

For days he pumped himself across the lake
to her—all rhythmic promise.
Only skim away to peck at rivals,
then stone-skip back to cruise in circles
as if she were the centre of his world.

What could she do—herself a regal model—
but dip her question mark, accept his offer.
He followed all the protocols.
His was the best dance on the lake that season
and the chill was coming.

Even now in autumn,
whenever a young male ripples by,
he flaps across the water, puffing up,
still the consummate performer
though his silhouette's thinner.

So there it is—the past—
a shadow play on the trees and ponds
reminding her why she took a chance.
He might be too in love with his reflection,
but oh, how he could dance!

## Jennifer Liston

### Egg

I take an almond-brown egg from the fridge.
Hello, egg.
Into almost-boiling water you go.
There you are, bobbing and twisting.
No use trying to escape.
Off what free range did you spring?
I'm told not to put you all in one basket.
You, potential sunny-side-up-runny-yoked half-life.
What chicken will you not become?
Your chocolate siblings dispersed at easter
by commercially cute button-nosed bunnies.
All the eggs in my womb basket
already broken,
devoured,
disgorged.
What boy or girl did they not become?
No sad Hallmark verses marked that occasion.
An almond-brown man I know
ate a raw egg daily.
He's 80.
Egg,
your time is up.

# Max Merckenschlager

## Channelled Energy

Jump in back, you kids
up in back o' ute, under tarp.
Quiet now, like little
Tadpoles—no, not wrigglers!
Police might catch us.
Too many tadpoles
no seat belts.

OK, all out!
Here—take them strings and bait.
Watch us catch them
yabbies in channel
Wall Flat channel.
Now you kids!

Jimmy, you got some?
*Yeahs, three. But need thirteen.*
*Promised thirteen*
*old ladies. Yabbies been ordered.*
*Saving biggest but*
*for my grandmother!*

You kids done all right
today. Better than
makin' trouble in town, aina?
Trouble is, gove'nment filling
them channels soon.
No yabbies then, eh kids?

# Ed Moreno

## When Pigs Fly

A pig flew over the Battersea Power Station. I've seen the photos. It flew as far as Kent, a distance of 74 kilometres, and flights to Heathrow had to be diverted for safety reasons. This is fact. It happens oftener than you think, considering the offhand way we use the phrase, believing ourselves exempted from having to do some god-awful thing or other: extend an apology, lift a finger. I've seen pigs in blankets stretch their wings. This is based in fact, although now I'm taking some poetic liberties. I had to shuttle our next-door neighbour Roz and her two-hundred-year-old sister Rue around for a day after those little sausages took flight. They beat their puff pastry wings like mad, heading off over the fence, and away from my dinner plate. Behind the wheel of Roz's Dodge, I cursed those wursts and scanned the sidewalks for anything even slightly interesting. I saw a mailbox shaped like a bi-winged pig in flight. It caught my eye, and I came back a week later in the middle of the night, smashed, and sent that mailbox flying with an aluminium baseball bat, an angry teen. That mailbox, and many others. This is fact. So there you have three instances of flying pigs, and in just a single paragraph. This is fact.

I still get fired up over things, little things. Anything, many things. When I get ejected from bars these days it takes five bouncers to get me out the door, the way I carry on. And I'm just a little fella. Cuts and bruises, plenty. Jobs, lost. Bridges, burned. I should do something about my drinking: when pigs fly. I enjoy—too much to give it up—a bottle of red or white or amber, on my own, of an evening or an afternoon or a morning. It smoothes the edges, brings on sleep. It's only when other people are around that it's a problem. You could say it's their drinking problem. But this is about pigs, so I'll give you another example: on November 4, 1909, Lord Brabazon, holder of the first pilot's license in the UK, took a pig for a 3½ mile joyride in a biplane in a basket tied onto the plane's wing, bearing a sign that said 'I am the first pig to fly'. This is fact.

I could go on, but I've made my point. How about just one more for the road? Ok, here goes: I don't actually believe that pigs can fly, being a heavy animal without wings, but chew on this for a while: if they did would anything be different? Would I go out of my way to help someone? Would I smile more? Would you? I wonder. God grant me serenity. I could be a friendlier type, with a whistle on my lips, a wistful look in my eye, clean jeans, and a part in my hair. It could happen. This is fact.

# Nicola Scholes

## Question Dots

The pimples appear like questions ...
*Will I fit in? Will I make friends?*
*Does he like me ...?*
tiny ones, ones with little white question
dots ... dry ones ... whole galaxies of black
stars I wouldn't wish upon ... anyone.
It isn't long before
*What subjects should I choose?* develops
a succulent, juicy one ... plump ... begging
to burst. My brother scratches and scars
his stubbled beard, but I am skilled
in the art & precision of squeezing.
Sometimes it doesn't take much. A small
application of force, between fingertips.
It shoots like a pistol, snaps skin, a pin
prick of pain, oozing pleasure. I smile.
Wipe away the cream before the wine.
*Theatre. French.* This must be the best
and worst of adolescence.
Another squeeze ... better than chocolate
(is chocolate really an accessory?)
Twelve hours and two centimetres away
*What jobs will these lead to?*
an iceberg, slippery, stubborn ... shifting
and mutating, it circumnavigates my chin,
stretches my profile, perverts my smile.
It travels well—a tightly packed IKEA zit
in rose veneer.

Just before the year 12 formal I get pregnant
with quadruples ... *Will I get into uni?*
*What shall I study? Which uni? Where will I live?*
microscopic bellies magnified in
the future mirror. They weep easily.
Tingle with face wash. Sometimes they spray
answers like economical shower heads.
Other times they lay low, refuse to come clean.
If I could grasp
*What will my life be like?*
coax it to the surface ... glimpse just the tip
of its frightful plunge ...
that would be some consolation.
Instead, it lies dormant. Deep. Without a point
or a head. Lying low. I do not know
the extent of it.

# Ann Shenfield

## A bridge

In a crowded room she turns to you
and says: there's a bridge
that you're going to have to cross
this stranger who hints at angels

and who tells you her voices are saying,
*be careful, be careful* and it's like some fairytale
your grandmother might have told you
*—remember, don't stand out from the crowd*!

She is saying your eyes speak a language
of stray lucent signs but she's talking about angels
with voices and you standing on some bridge
that is for everyone to cross.

You're stuck in that conversation,
in that moment, that could be the present,
it's like a cry from the playground
that nobody else hears, and she's saying

—your eyes speak too much, they say you're alone
when you're in a crowded room, although there isn't
a room, there isn't even a crowd, there's just the hum
of a distant swell, under a bridge, where it all falls away.

## Anna Skeer

### Gum Leaves on a Windy Barossa Day

Glittering jewels tussle
At the tree top,
Turbid they tear away
On a drunken branch
Rolling over
Only to be yanked
Violently back
As the branch
Regains its composure.

Then they form lines
Seaweed in the swell
The south winds prevail
Slanting silver sideways.

A part in the comb-over
Exposes the bare
White backbones of the branches
And sunlight sharp
Highlights each jewel edge
Reminiscent of sunlight
Sparkling on brill cream.

# Alex Skovron

## Confutatis

When I glanced inside, the old musicians were hearsing again,
somebody's Nonth Symphony, in a key impossibly remote.

This, for some odd reason, infuriated me,
and the tableau's eerie intensity implied
that I surely was unawake.

Approaching the pedestal,
I drumrolled my baton with unseemly petulance, accosted
the snowy-headed first violin, who proceeded to quote
a major Roman poet.

'*Ira furor brevis est*,' the man epistled, and grinned atrociously.

Sensing a challenge, but fancying myself
a Latinist at heart,
'*Concordia discors*,' I shot back at once.
'And what, sir, is your name?'

He streaked a thumb among unruly locks
before returning with a lazy bow, 'Why,
Tierce de Picardie, though my friends call me Quintus.
What would you have us play?'

This gave me pause, but
'Something a bit more minor,' I replied at length,
'somebody's Fifth, perhaps?'

The fiddler scratched at his scroll,
regave another of his diabolical sneers. 'Oh no,
we couldn't do that!' he nodded catachrestically, 'not unless
the work is an Opus Zero. *Nil admirari*, you know ...'

(I might well have bristled at this, but my mood
had by now improved.)

With an immusical creak of knees
he regained his seat, to sound a lugubrious A.
The ragtag crew, disarranged on haphazard chairs,
ignoring me with thinly disguised wonder, shuffled
among their music-stations.

Interrogatively, I upturned my palms.
'*Da capo*,' the *ductor* intoned, and they embarked
on a *Tuba mirum* by somebody not yet born.

I glanced outside, but morning was still asleep.

# Ian C Smith

## Survival

She told me how ghost-haunted night passes
and in the pale lemon grey morning
she goes out as though nothing has changed
although sane enough to fear a future.
Evening comes and she discovers
where to buy bread and newspapers
milk and meat, climbs the stained stairs
takes possession, learns to light the gas
learns where to put things, where to sit
so she can read and eat at the same time.
She reads, lost in narrative, crumbs hardening
a tawny scum shrinking on her cold tea.
Finally she ventures on her first night prowl
mapping the shadowy neighbourhood
learning at each turn, then retraces her steps
reads again, and later settles to sleep.
Next morning she wakes to a routine
for the first time, goes off to work
to her new job where she is not known.
No-one has this address, there is no phone
just these blackened bricks, exhaust fumes.
She works, repeats her necessary purchases
manages her routine with less conscious effort.
Night follows night and brings familiarity
until she begins to think at last
of what brought her here to this place.
Rain drenches the black city outside
as she pushes aside unwashed plates
revolves a pen between her fingers
cracks open the journal she has bought.

# Jessica Szwarcbord

## Excavation

I curl myself up like a ferret to watch 'The Sound of Music',
While the rain tumbles down around me and drums upon my whirring thoughts,
Like the little drummer-boy I saw outside Le Grand Palais one winter,
All these intrusive droplets seen through the Perspex windows of my bell-jar house.

I should hang curtains up for this new season of ice and fearfully beautiful thunder,
But then I would be building a brick cage in line with the glass,
Doubling the wall of my already solidified burrow so I could no longer see beyond,
To the world I so carefully keep beyond reach of my delicate fingertips,

The world is so much—so intense that touching it directly is like being tickled;
Wonderful, yet impossible to bear for more than a few seconds,
For fear of being overwhelmed by its intensity and wondrous light,
Yes, Destoievski: collective harmony is frightening when it becomes crystal,

So I've built my nest with glass walls to dull the shock but keep connected to people,
Rushing past, as I look through café windows, at jobs and lovers and children,
Jobs where they calculate numbers until eyes glaze over,
And lovers who say more in the days they don't call than in whispered romances,

Children run to school, to piano class and to pick up forgotten bikes,
Bikes left under trees in parks when a mother discovers their child out in the cold,
'Without a jacket, you'll get a cold!' and pulls them home by the collar,
While I sit under an opposite tree with an umbrella to make me invisible,

Sometimes I snap into a trance and long to walk through streets without an umbrella,
And I flash outside in a flurry without a jumper, having forgotten it's 10 degrees,
Until I get back and take off my coat realising I should have been cold,
But in too much awe at the magnificence of every shade of colour to mind,

And the glass breaks because I no longer need it,
And I put up curtains because I know I can always push them aside,
And I throw myself into a world of jobs and lovers and children,
And I remain in a bell-jar of my own space and time,

I begin a routine so I may function in this functioning world,
I begin to love others for highlighting what I'm not,
I remain like a child—holding tight to those wonders,
Which, like gems, remain buried for all save those who excavate them.

## Jenny Toune

### Renovation

1982. My head had barely touched the pillow
than it was off again. Ontological studies abandoned
speed dominates thought
/ contemplation
no musing but one brief flicker
is nirvana the silence or the pulse?
(not that I had experienced the silence
but the pulse was euphoric).

2002. Fingers
wrapped in head
/ space
unwilling to regard the cessation
of life lines
with anything approaching sober consideration.
Empty rooms echo solo flight
I wash the sand from my eyes
turn again.
Ontological studies resume ...
I discover
the pulse is just a heartbeat.

Now ... everyone I know is renovating
dream homes usurp dream life
in the silent
                    / golden years.
Even I feel the pull to polyfill ...
do we all end up fussing over real estate
                                        no matter which road we've travelled?

## Amelia Walker

### Just Your Everyday Apocalypse

The tide has come in so much since this morning, when I was just six years old.
It has swallowed the shoreline—just rocks now, no sand,
then bitumen and houses, brown front lawns curling like nervous toes.
I've become older, much older than twenty three—the age I am. Funny
how a one week visit to my parents can entwine so many years and eras.

It was 1983 when I stepped off the plane,
by that evening Dodos filled the garden and none of us were born
—which made conversation a curiosity, oddly full of ease.
The next morning I woke beneath the rubble of the Berlin Wall.
My father showed me how to tie a tie and I cried because it was so easy,
one more piece of knowledge that no longer made him special.
But over breakfast we forgot about gravity and Earth being round
and pancakes tasted all the better for their miracle return to the pan.
My grandfather sailed straight through the ceiling with a pink and gold parachute,
my mother believed in Santa—until Australia sent troops to Vietnam
and then there were no frogs anywhere on Earth.
We argued about what I'd wear to the school formal,
by noon I'd moved out of home for the first time, by dinner I was back
floating marshmallows in a mug of hot chocolate, I'd never been kissed.

That night was the hottest on record in twenty three years. Nobody slept.
It was 4 am for days. At 5 am my mother gave birth to my sister
so I wasn't an only child anymore. She was a fussy eater who topped every exam
and brought her washing home for Mum to do long after she'd moved out.
Just when we thought she'd never lose that Goth make up
she smiled and said her first word. By mid day she had her PhD.
Meanwhile, Mum was still asking me what I planned to do when I grew up

—I was fifty years old and hadn't stayed in one job longer than twelve months.
Over dinner I told them my marriage was over.
Mum kept on shoving mashed banana into my mouth until I spat it
all over her white blouse and howled that I loved a woman.
Then two planes slammed into the twin towers
ten minutes after we went right to the top of them on our family holiday in 1993.
Australia sent troops into Iraq, and then there were no trees anywhere on Earth.

I stared at the setting sun until I went blind, then stumbled the dark streets all night
until I blinked and found myself between starched sheets, wearing a white gown.
The doctor scolded, the nurse brought chalk.
Mum visited, sat me on her knee and said the soul is something like a blackboard.
I was discharged that afternoon and began learning to read.
I turned twenty one, I turned three, my grandfather died, I turned eighteen,
God left and I wrote in my journal *I can't kill myself because I'm already dead.*
Then I slept for two years and woke up smiling because I'd realised
something can disappear from your sight without ceasing to exist.

At sunrise my grandmother invented fire, my parents fell in love,
the fighting stopped, rain came, all famines ended, I was born
by caesarean section, strong and kicking despite predictions I wouldn't make it.
I have made it, now, to the place where this path ends
—though the ocean, of course, continues. It is sundown
on the sixth day of this visit. I decided to move interstate
—job opportunity—my mother's howls still carry on the wind,
dancing with the grumblings of Krakatoa, who has woken with a hangover
spewing fire. Polar bears are drowning, Gondwanaland splitting apart.
One day it will be possible for every man to own his own car.
The houses with their lawns are gone now. The sea is turning
red, gold, green, brown—a bruise, trapped blood turning sour.
I hold my own baby daughter's ancient, dying hand,
whisper tales of days when it was clean enough to swim.

# John Watson

## Cloud Studies

1 Clouds like tea unstirred,
The milk added last.

2 A swathe of clouds.

3 Clouds like contour ploughing.

4 Clouds of the many
Forms already familiar from
The history of painting.

5 Clouds like eroded creekbeds
Where young saplings grow.

6 Notes to the above.

In 2, assume tulle
Or organza over shoulders
As white as clouds.

In 4, the sky
Admittedly does sometimes seem
At pains to show
Many configurations at once.

In 5, is there
Some suggestion or memory
Of a mirror dam
Waiting for its cloud?

Or is 'young samplings'
Simply an affectionate memory
Of the map scene
In Olivier's *Uncle Vanya*?

And are the clouds
Unrolling and vanishing before
Likenesses can be verified?

7 Some which have been
Unnoticed by everyone sunbathing.

8 Some which only now
Cast their grey gauze
Over some estuary fishermen.

9 Clouds plied and implied.

10 Where some clouds dissolve,
Note suggestions of lattice
Or even a hint
Of light involuntarily polarised.

11 Ploughed field cloud irises
Scanned on outbound shallows.

12 Clouds like sheets washed
In the river, then
Twisted on the bank.

13 One sort of cloud
With another beside it,
The two generously linked
By a mile high
Cone of lemon gelato.

14 Further notes: 'Cloud irises'
Must almost certainly refer
To the blue gaps
Reflected in the river.

'Ploughing' is remarkably prevalent
In accounts of clouds
Suggesting some closer affinity
Between earth and sky
Than is generally apparent.

# Identity and Its Double

## The Variable River

On one of his many excursions
To and from the variable river
Heraclitus brings back a bucket
Of river water. It sits
In his room for a few days
Until he deems it settled,
Then proclaims, *Now I'll dip my hands*
*Twice into the same river.*

## From Callimachus

They told me, Heraclitus, you had died.
The bitter messages arrived today
And since the faltering moment I have shed
A river-flood of tears. For you and I
Would often, and with such delight, sustain
An anabranch of words with tributaries,
Diversions, loops and streams, so that the sun
In weariness would sink below the trees.

Death takes you from me, yet cannot erase
Your many voices, those sweet nightingales
Mellifluous and infinitely wise.
And now you step once only into shoals
Of that same river, pausing at this shore,
Which at a distance flows past every door.

## On Displacement

In Sebald's *Vertigo* one reads that Beyle
Held pessimistic views of Memory.
This Henri Beyle, who blossoms as Stendhal,
Had treasured memories of Italy
Which, after many years, had proved to be
An echo of some copy he had seen.
These had, he found, erased true memory
And left instead a false, conventional scene.

He found he had no accurate recall
Of certain masterpieces; in their place,
Some poor engraving muffled every trace.
He warns the traveller: do not build that wall
In front of memory. Look at the leaf,
The face, the tree, but take no photograph.

## In the Footsteps of Morandi

The Via Fondazza gardens
Eventually to be ruined
By real estate speculators
Were for his lifetime

Still breathing and growing,
Their suspiration faintly heard
From his little bed,
Their almost unchanging clusters

Visible from his window.
A wall encroached upon
A narrow path blindly
Pursuing its course between

Cypress and bay trees
A few steps away
Stood his easel encrusted
With paint and, everywhere

Round it, spattered paint—
Everywhere, that is, except
For the twin footprints,
Unchanging, where he stood.

## Les Wicks

### The Sex Madness

I know
when your head is all hole. Boys' School
council pool
dive into your drink.
I once groped a curtain.
You did too.

We spark in the dust. Regency
of muck-energy, the punch.
Call it love, cut the foreskin then
give it to gods.

Girls are the contradiction of cloud.
One follows the clouds.

I understood, but couldn't share
the edge of hate.
They **are** laughing at us
                                        on the bus
                              beneath intemperate sun
      as they drive past in the bare skin of their cars.

Flounce plastic. Crushed grass,
beasts harden for the entertainment of glands.
In the debrief
we sniff each others' fingers.

Might isn't right hemisphere.
Knuckled print and breeding fall,
We'll sell our bones for silence.

For some, it's a temporary teenage indigestion.
A few choke in smoke all life. There's
those accidents of ethics and inhibition
that place us within the simulacrum of normality.
It's a gut thing, spirit.
In the young all patience, grace
would be a waste.

You'll get your taste
stretched on the time,
reptile sun. Hold on, escape.
the impossible want,
improbable delay.

Avoid the firestorm,
sirocco years will settle to
somewhere between a scab and a ruby...
be enough. Easy to say 'endure', but
with a few deep breathes you will.

We will always
have the privilege
to be waiting for women.

Jena Woodhouse

## The house at Mervyn Grove

You don't remember your first year,
our evenings on the balcony,
the buzz of voices from below
as husbands became bachelors,
and visitors were jocular
exotic men, whose origins were far
removed from that genteel
suburban grove, whose *lingua franca*
was the billiard cue, the *pok* of balls
on wood, the green felt melting
boundaries (though not including
balconies), while womenfolk
watched TV shows and chatted
in their mother tongue, and I,
the stranger in their midst,
uncomprehendingly looked on.

The carp swam in their lily pond
like globules rising in the bar-lamp,
as the young men lounged about
the pool table and joked and smoked.

This was their gilded ghetto,
where the outside world was kept at bay,
and meals came sizzling with steamy
gastronomic Shanghai ghosts.
Only I could not join in
the chatter of the family—the blue-eyed
stranger in their midst, a gauche anomaly.

The kitchen hissed with pans
and thudding, crunching, violent
chopping sounds, the sole domain
of agile hands, a scraped-back bun,
a toothy grin. The master smiled,
a crocodile. Was she, the cook,
his concubine?
Now they've toned it Tuscan ochre,
that mansion in Mervyn Grove,
and the woman with her hose
has no idea, we may suppose,
of who lived there for many moons,
or what they wore, or how they loved;
the narratives that linked those rooms,
and what their grieves and secrets were ...

*

You should not have had to learn
impermanence so young;

the gaunt, shape-shifting ways of loss,
the alphabet of pain.

Now I hear that you're about to move
out of that seaside flat,

where gulls plane past the windows
as the first light rolls in from the east,

and all the rooms are clepsydras
replenished by the Bondi sun,

and Evie, who has just turned one,
runs clutching at its rays ...

*for Larisa*
from the sequence *The Book of Lost Addresses*

# Poetics

Ffion Murphy

## Stingo's Choice: Reflections on Judgement, Selection and Rejection

Recently, and in the wake of reading hundreds of entries submitted for the 2007 Max Harris Poetry Award, I re-read the opening chapter of William Styron's 1979 novel *Sophie's Choice*. What drew me to select this title from my cluttered bookshelves I cannot say for certain, but Styron's depiction of an arrogant junior editor's belligerent criticism and ebullient rejection of manuscripts submitted for publication recalled for me the frustrations, cruelties and erotics of writing, reading and reviewing. Perhaps it was simply the book's title that attracted attention: its focus on 'choice', and its opening chapter's reminder that choosing can be a devilish business, and being rejected in publishing, as in love, might break one's heart. Of course, drawing an analogy between Sophie's choice and the young editor Stingo's (or any editor's or literary judge's) seems flawed, even contemptible. Sophie's choice must rank amongst the most painful of any depicted in Western literature and is of a different order. Who can forget the drunken doctor's words to the stricken mother as he selects candidates for Birkenau: 'You're a Pollack, not a Yid. That gives you a privilege—a choice' (Styron 1992, p. 642). Choosing which of your two young children must certainly die in a Nazi gas chamber is not equivalent to choosing who will receive a publishing contract or a prize, along with a modicum of glory, for their particular ordering of marks on a white page.

How interesting, then, that Styron's extraordinary novel opens by describing young Stingo's revulsion at bad writing and disillusion with the job of manuscript assessor, which, contrary to his expectations, turns out to be neither gripping nor glamorous. The publishing company that employs him dabbles in nonfiction and fiction, but prospers mostly by producing textbooks, manuals, and technical journals. Though dealing with the literary side of things, Stingo finds there is little to compensate for his meagre earnings of ninety cents per hour. He plods through fiction and nonfiction of the 'humblest possible quality—coffee-stained and thumb-smeared stacks of Hammerhill Bond'. Narrating his experience as a successful writer thirty years later, Stingo concedes that he was 'savagely demanding' and admits that he relished producing 'callous reader's reports' (1992, p. 12) for the senior editor in which he 'eviscerated' writers easily dismissed as 'helpless, underprivileged, subliterary lambkins' (1992, p. 13):

> I treated these forlorn offspring of a thousand strangers' lonely and fragile desire with the magisterial, abstract loathing of an ape plucking vermin from his pelt. I was adamant, cutting, remorseless, insufferable ... I levelled the scorn that could only be mustered by one who had just finished reading *Seven Types of Ambiguity* upon these sad outpourings piled high on my desk, all of them so freighted with hope and clubfooted syntax. (1992, p. 12)

Stingo does not recall recommending a single manuscript for publication during his five months of employment with McGraw-Hill. Some of his reader reports are included and they are scathing. Styron indicated in an interview that while he drew closely on his own experience at McGraw-Hill for the opening section, the reader reports in the novel are fictional (Armes 1979, p. 3).

Stingo's editorial disdain is amusing. But as I nod and chuckle, recalling similarly disparaging remarks heard from the lips of some real-life editors, as well as some English and writing teachers, I recognise the baseness of this response and admit that the sequence also has me squirming, just a little. The excruciating comedy crafted by Styron is of the 'slipped on a banana skin' variety, surely. One does not wish to be the clubfooted fool splayed on the parquetry. Styron would no doubt have been aware how many writer 'wannabes' exist and how many readers are potentially rejected writers. Arguably there are many more rejected writers now than there were in the late 1970s when he published the novel (though he couldn't have imagined that a 2008 Google search would find over half a million internet sites for 'literary rejection' alone). Styron might also have suspected that many editors and publishing personnel would gleefully identify with Stingo—how gratifying to find their plight, their *burden*, so vividly dramatised and to imagine all those worthless and time-wasting submissions being ruthlessly vanquished. Perhaps some junior assessors secretly yearn for a tolerant senior editor like Stingo's, who does not seek to curb a novice's excesses. But then, in the evenings when they take up their pens to scribble their novels or poems, do they begin to tremble and waver? Do they begin to imagine his scorn being levelled at them?

Stingo is perhaps entitled to enjoy his moment of superiority, gained by a 'snootful of English Lit.' education (1992, p. 12). I'm not sure how anyone who seriously tries to write poetry, fiction or nonfiction with a view to publication can remain insufferable when called upon to judge other people's words. The parental metaphor Stingo adapts is familiar and resonant—the manuscripts he must read are other people's 'forlorn offspring'—but this should serve as a warning. Writing, it is often said, involves conception, incubation, labour and birth. *Voila*: the writing is the baby. The parent/writer is inevitably protective of this precious addition to the world, and invested in its survival, and more, its success.

I recall a particular sentence of French from my fat secondary school textbook: 'Qu'il est laid, ce bébé'. As a teenager I found it extraordinary that we would be encouraged to learn how to say 'What an ugly baby', for when could we possibly use it? Imagine: we pause by a pram parked on the Metro platform and, after peering in, look up at the proud, grinning parent and murmur that practised tribute ... I mention this because while it is possible that this baby *is* ugly, and that many others are too, it cannot be guaranteed that parents will share such views: on the contrary, they will see beauty in the child, perhaps in his mystical pallor, or in the statement made by her remarkable ears. In other words, we unwillingly recognise shortcomings in our offspring, and generally resent having them pointed out by others. Furthermore, advice that your child's nose is bulbous does not necessarily help: once you're over denying it, and grudgingly concede the case, you need access to methods—surgical or otherwise—that might remedy the situation.

It is easy enough to be flippant. But returning to the question of Styron's motivation for placing Stingo's editorial experience at the beginning of a novel concerning the abomination of Nazism, and further attention to his word choice, suggests he is drawing a parallel after all, and this is a serious matter. As part of a publishing company of 'regimented minions' (1992, p. 29), Stingo revels in dispensing judgement on others' offspring—'with the magisterial, abstract loathing of an ape plucking vermin from his pelt' (1992, p. 12). This description is surely meant to prefigure descriptions of Nazi behaviour. Later in life, Stingo treasures just one of his reader's reports because 'it may have been the only one [he] wrote containing anything resembling compassion' (1992, p. 15). The manuscript, delivered to Stingo in person, had taken its author twenty years to write. Stingo is initially sceptical, as is his habit, but becomes intrigued by the author, an intelligent, 'very articulate' and well read wheat farmer, whose epic poem is based on one of his Norwegian ancestors. He wonders if he might discover 'some sort of rough-hewn genius' for, after all, 'even a great poet like Whitman came on like a clumsy oddball, peddling his oafish script everywhere' (1992, p. 17). Unfortunately, though, this manuscript too must be declined.

If we have any doubt about Styron's intentions in this opening chapter, they might be dispelled by his narrator's disparaging comments on the publishing company that employed him: 'McGraw-Hill was, after all, in spite of its earnest literary veneer, a monstrous paradigm of American business' (1992, p. 28). Styron forces a comparison between stultifying corporate capitalism and fascist authoritarian anti-humanism, neither of which can stomach individualism or diversity. This becomes especially evident when a new editor-in-chief, a 'cold company man' nicknamed Weasel, makes it clear that Stingo fails to fit the company 'profile': 'Everyone at McGraw-Hill wears a hat,' he tells Stingo (1992, p. 29). Every man wears a hat, that is, except Stingo, who also reads the wrong newspaper at lunchtimes, one which bespeaks radicalism when even sensationalism would be preferable. Stingo comes to believe, though, that Weasel is the 'true prisoner of Mc-Graw Hill, irrevocably committed to its pettifoggery and its mean-spirited style' (1992, p. 30). Farrell, the senior editor, is also a kind of prisoner, a man who once aspired to be a writer but who now suffers from the 'McGraw-Hill syndrome of despair and attrition' (1992, p. 22). In sympathy with Stingo's departure from the company, he uses a metaphor of release that again prefigures the novel's concern with forms of physical and mental entrapment and abuses of power: 'A narrow escape ... People have been known to drown in this place. And they never even find their bodies' (1992, p. 32).

Stingo is confronted, finally, with a choice: to become like Weasel or Farrell or to don the 'soaring wings' of his favourite authors—at the end of the chapter he comments that hearing Farrell's sad story struck him so deeply that he became aware of the 'large hollowness' (1992, p. 39) he carried within him. This language and the story of doomed, trapped men may recall TS Eliot's poem 'The Hollow Men', and its reference to the shadow that falls between action and inaction, being or not being fully alive, answering or not answering the call, which, in Stingo's case, comes from writers such as Tolstoy, Melville, Fitzgerald, or Flaubert who 'each night, separately and together, were summoning [him] to their incomparable vocation' (1992, pp. 22-23). Uniformity, commercialism—in this romantic discourse these are anathema to creativity.

Once Stingo realises his days with the publisher are numbered, he is 'able to play, in this fortress of white Anglo-Saxon power, the dual role of imaginary Communist and fictive Jew' (1992, p. 31). This reference to Jews is not the first: in the novel's opening paragraph Stingo refers to his self-exile 'like others of my countrymen, another lean and lonesome young Southerner wandering amid the Kingdom of the Jews' (1992, p. 9). This alliance makes for an interesting volte-face, because Stingo, in taking employment with a major publisher, changes from self-styled wanderer to something akin to a Nazi victimiser (of writers), and then into a disinherited survivor who enacts a final 'gesture of defection' for which he will be sacked on the spot. His expulsion is a form of birth, of deliverance into writing; Stingo is propelled out of an oppressive, onanistic state into the messy post-war world, where he will encounter love, passion, madness and death in a necessary 'voyage of discovery' (1992, p. 39).

Stingo claims that as a young man he had an 'affinity for the written word—almost any written word, that was so excitable that it verged on the erotic' (1992, p. 21). Trying to write book blurbs alone in his meagre room at night, he is filled with a sense of degradation: 'I would pace my cell distractedly, uttering soft meaningless vocables to the air as I struggled with the prose rhythms, and fighting back the desolate urge to masturbate that for some reason always accompanied this task' (1992, p. 23). The words finally come when he is overwhelmed by rage, but they are not words that will please the publisher. The literary and sexual relate in fascinating ways, the novel suggests. Writing and reading arise from and promote desire—fragile, potent, unruly, vain ... What editor or literary judge has not felt that tingle of excitement on picking up a new submission? Or frustration when it disappoints? Or a rush when encountering something marvellous? Stingo's impossible lust when alone in his single room translates into fierce rejection of others when he is at his editor's desk.

At the end of the chapter, the narrator reflects: 'I was too young to be really afraid of much but not so young that I remained unshaken by certain apprehensions. Those ludicrous manuscripts I had read were somehow cautionary, showing me how sad was all ambition—especially when it came to literature' (1992, p. 38). There is an odd tension here between publishing and editing as a monstrous business, deadening for its conformity and banality, its cruelty and its products, and notions of the writer as necessarily independent and free-spirited: Stingo learned early in life that he 'would never fit in as an office worker, anytime, anywhere' (1992, p. 10). Wanting 'beyond hope or dreaming to be a writer' and escaping routine work is fine for literary stalwarts like Stingo, but not, it seems, for those whose work he deems ludicrous (1992, p. 38).

In *A History of Reading*, Alberto Manguel (1997) relates an anecdote told by Claude Lévi-Strauss, whose hosts for a while, the Nambikwara Indians of Brazil, watched curiously as he wrote his notes; they then took his pencil and paper and drew squiggles in imitation, before demanding that he read them: 'The Nambikwara expected their scribbles to be as immediately significant to Lévi-Strauss as those he drew himself'. However, for Lévi-Strauss, who was 'taught to read in a European school, the notion that a system of communication should be immediately comprehensible to any other person seemed absurd' (1997, p. 67). More worrying, perhaps, is the realisation that even when we *do* share a system of communication, readers very often fail to find a writer's words 'immediately significant' or even remotely affecting or interesting, despite the writer's hopes and intentions.

Thomas Keneally aptly sums up the problem of recognition and validation in an interview published in *Making Stories: How Ten Australian Novels Were Written*: 'What I've noticed over a long career is that writers' assessments of what's working and what isn't [are] abysmal; it's very subjective and quite unreliable. The [writer's] exaltation can attach itself as easily to a weed as to a rose' (Woolf & Grenville 1993, p. 195). A writer whose work has been deemed a weed and rejected might counter by insisting that weeds are not born but designated: no species is innately second-rate, but is repudiated because it tends to proliferate without human encouragement where it is not wanted. Editors and gardeners might respond that weeds sometimes do have off-putting characteristics: prickles, spines, hairs, poisonous sap, thorns ... It is quite usual to hear editors and judges use the metaphor of weeding out unsuitable manuscripts. In *Creative Writing: A Practical Guide*, for example, Julia Casterton (2005) reassures writers that if they've entered lots of competitions but never won anything it might not be because their writing is poor. She adds:

> Remember that the main judges don't see the bulk of the entries because the competition organisers weed them out beforehand. In a sense, the competition is judged even before it is judged. Philip Larkin, in his book *Required Writing*, tells a peculiar story about judging a competition where there were no love poems or nature poems. He asked the organisers 'Where are the love and nature poems?' and they replied 'Oh, we weeded them out'. (2005, p. 176)

As far as I know, the judges of most literary competitions in Australia read all correctly submitted entries—as in the case of the Max Harris Poetry Award—so the judges do all the weeding themselves. But, how appropriate is this term?

Manguel suggests that '[a]ll writing depends on the generosity of the reader' (1997, p. 179), to make the point that texts are silent until read and attributed meaning. We might give his words a slightly different import, and add that writing also depends on the *respect* of the reader. And yet readerly generosity and respect seem easily dispensed with, and are reserved for particular kinds of writing within particular contexts.

Stingo's attitude is not surprising and peculiar to him but, rather, is all too recognisable and historically established. It is evident, for example, in a 1902 *New York Times* Review of Books and Art editorial titled 'Rejected Manuscripts' (1902, p. BR10). The column refers initially to comments published by Henry M Alden in the Editor's Study section of *Harper's Magazine*, which itself refers to comments made decades earlier by Charles Dickens in a letter to Mrs Gaskell. Describing the vast majority of manuscripts he rejects as editor of *Household Words*, Dickens complained:

> They are of that intensely dreary and commonplace description to which not even the experience of this place reconciles my wondering mind. Everybody could write such things, I imagine: but how anybody can contentedly sit down to do it is inscrutable ... People don't plunge into churches and play the organ without knowing the notes or having the ghost of an ear. Yet fifty people to-day will rush into manuscript, for these leaves only, who have no earthly qualifications but the actual physical art of writing ... I am at this moment sitting (up to the neck) in a quagmire of these productions. (Dickens cited in *New York Times* 1902, p. BR10)

Dickens initiated the weekly *Household Words* in 1850, and remained its editor for nine years before merging it into a similar periodical titled *All the Year Around.*[1] Many contributions were printed anonymously, but that did not seem to deter writers. Dickens selected a mix of topical and issues-based articles, a story, a poem, an essay, all designed to appeal to a growing popular or middle-class readership. According to biographer Peter Ackroyd the circulation settled to around 39,000, which was much less than some of the better established, more weighty periodicals but enough to 'generate a reasonable profit' (1990, p. 591).

Ackroyd points to expanding literacy as an important factor in the viability of periodicals such as *Household Words*: it took its place 'among the magazines which heralded or exploited the growth of the reading public throughout this period' (1990, p. 591). Growing literacy, of course, also encouraged the emergence of a writing public. The derision this public conjures from their first and possibly last readers seems due largely to their presumption: how dare they seek to be *authors*!

An article published in 1879 in the *New York Times* suggests that part of the problem is the growing number of women deluded into thinking that 'writing is an easy, if not fascinating, way of supporting one's self' (*New York Times* 1879, p. 6). The success of a few, such as Charlotte Bronte and Mrs Stowe, had misled some of 'narrow means' into thinking that they, too, might profit by publishing. The article discusses a few successful women to conclude:

> These examples show how women have succeeded as writers who are born for that vocation, and find their way to it by natural gravitation, but they give no encouragement to the venturesome ones who try to become authors because they can do nothing else. We should not dare to think of the amount of manuscript rejected by magazines which is now pigeonholed in many a private desk in all parts of the country—the result of the idea that anybody can write, whether bred to it or not, or the effort of worthy but mistaken women to earn a pittance by writing miserable stories, and more miserable poems. (1879, p. 6)

The article claims that there will be terrible disappointment among those who have 'mistaken their ability to write and are in the depths of poverty', adding that the 'persistence of many women is in inverse ratio to their ability to write what the public will read' (1879, p. 6). The writer lauds editors who protect the public from 'this literary deluge', but this is somewhat disingenuous, because such editors, presuming the women's writing will not appeal, never give the public a chance to judge. Perhaps the women's stories would not have appealed to the paper's male readers, but might women readers have enjoyed stories by other women? It is worth quoting the article's advice:

> We do not wish to debar the gentler sex from the field of authorship; far from it. Women can never do the largest or highest work in literature because they are not fitted for it and men cannot do the choice and precious work that belongs almost exclusively to woman; but it is best for the public, best for the parties themselves, that ten thousand excellent and needy women shall not seek to make a living by what they write when they have nothing to say. We would like to say to these fair ones: 'Please don't write anything; do something; make a place for yourself with your hands; don't inflict your thoughts upon other people ... ' (1879, p. 6)

The article argues that 'no woman, without the training which teaches one how to say something, and without the personal experience which gives one something to say, can expect to do anything creditable to herself ...' The questions of being born to write, or of 'training', though, are decidedly vexed, and so while it is easy enough in the twenty-first century to scoff at such patriarchal nonsense, and to assert that one of any gender, race, class or creed is equally entitled to write, I suspect we have not progressed so far in answering the question of what qualifications produce a publishable writer.

Dickens's observation that many submissions to his periodical are from those with 'no earthly qualifications' to write might suggest that tertiary and other courses established the following century precisely so that those managing the physical act of writing could also learn the art of publishable writing would be universally applauded, and especially appreciated by editors, reviewers, and other literary 'judges'. This is not always so. Over several years now I have fumed at newspaper articles that question the legitimacy of university writing courses, and reviews of novels and poetry that denigrate the writers and often the work largely because the writer has done a writing course, and such courses have also been blamed for the 'deluge' that continues to bother publishers. There is not the scope here to elaborate on such a perverse occurrence, or to consider the way that being schooled in one's chosen practice becomes in such discourse a threat to an elusive god-given gift, vital artistic sensibility, or vivid lived experience, but only to say that the 'novice' writer remains too easy a target for the 'expert' reader's derision.

Fifty years after Dickens wrote of being inundated with the dreary and commonplace, the 1902 *New York Times* article surmised that the number of 'aspiring authors who possess no qualification for authorship except the ability to write grammatically must have greatly increased with the spread of common school education both in England and America' (1902, p. BR10). Education was not only spreading among women, but also in colonial outposts, and this would produce yet more people—some without full mastery of conventional English grammar and syntax—with the effrontery to submit their work to publishers.

The odds of publication fifty years apart and on different sides of the Atlantic were appalling, and clearly remain so. Dickens wrote a lot of material for *Household Words*, especially in its early years, but also worked hard as an editor of other people's submissions. In 1852, he estimated that he read 900 manuscripts 'of which only 11 were suitable for publication', and that was after 'substantial rewriting by himself' (Ackroyd 1990, p. 591).

The *New York Times* estimated in 1902 that *Harper's Magazine* received 50 manuscripts a day, and that 'perhaps once a year, maybe not so often, the first offering of an author is accepted'. According to Alden, the article notes, the one who wins against so much competition 'shows his or her merit in the earliest offerings' (1902, p. BR10). But an equally disquieting observation follows—that the promise of even the better manuscripts is often not fulfilled: 'We may assume that ten or twelve thousand persons contribute manuscripts to the magazine every year which are rejected. Of these a small proportion may find a market elsewhere'. The article also asserts that 'the number of aspirants for literary fame is ever on the increase', but uses the word 'fame' speciously for it goes on to note that '[t]he reward of success is small, the discouragement disheartening, but the deluge continues' (1902, p. BR10).

Quagmire? Deluge? These common descriptors are hyperbolic, but clearly reflect the sense some editors have of being overwhelmed as if by natural disasters. The *New York Times* is unrelenting, and makes it clear that too much bad writing is a problem across the board, and is not confined to particular genres or publishing outlets:

> We know to our sorrow that the number of persons of both sexes who consider themselves competent to write about literature is as large as if not larger than the number who hopelessly assail the magazine editors ... The situation is both painful and puzzling. The age is full of alertness and practicality, and there are so many more useful and profitable things to do than writing manuscripts which are read only by the editors who do not want them. (1902, p. BR10)

Editors aren't entirely unsympathetic to the plight of writerly aspirants, but their own discomfort, their sense of being assailed by others' dreams and unable to do anything but disappoint them, is clearly wearying.

Judges of literary competitions may feel similarly overwhelmed. It must be assumed that every entrant believes winning is possible, perhaps especially where they have paid a fee to be considered. And judges today, like editors, no doubt relate to the exasperation expressed by their forerunners. My purpose in raising this issue is not to protest that any rejected writing is worthy of prizes or publication, nor to demonise editors and publishers by suggesting that their judgements are always heartless and ill-considered; after all, most surely want nothing more than to receive and publish good and interesting material, and most are polite in their communications with writers. Furthermore, many editors are also writers, or aspiring writers, and appreciate the difficulties of writing and the harshness of rejection. My concern is, rather, with the flippant or hostile attitude of some professional readers, judges, editors, and teachers towards submissions deemed unfit for publication and the glib communication of such attitudes among themselves and in general reportage.

If Stingo's account is not enough to remind us of the unhealthy relationship that potentially inheres between assessors and writers, here's another and older example. In America in 1862 a writers' competition was established in an effort to find a United States National Hymn, and it attracted nearly 1200 competitors, all of whom, according to a *New York Daily Times* report reprinted in *The Musical World*, would be 'sitting upon the anxious seat' (1862, p. 12) along with their friends and families while awaiting the result. The report examines the selection process, and interesting parallels can be seen with contemporary practices, except that the committee of judges was to look for a submission that exactly suited its purposes, not just the 'best' submitted. It considered words-only manuscripts first (about 900 entries). Each entry was read by the committee member who first received it, and then passed to the others. If the entry was 'condemned by most', then it was 'caste into a waste-basket ready at hand'. Interestingly the columnist does not stop there, but instead elaborates rather pompously on the nature of the basket:

> But, by waste-basket must not be understood any of those wicker concavities, known to ordinary mortals by that name. A vast washing-basket—a 'bulk-basket', being enough to hold Falstaff himself—was made the temporary tomb of these extinguished hopes; and this receptacle was filled, it is said, five times with rejected manuscripts, which were seized upon for incendiary purposes by the cooks of the gentlemen at whose houses the meetings of the Committee took place. Alas for the hapless writers! Were even the priceless manuscript plays of the Shakespearian age that Warburton's cook purloined and used to put under pies so lamented as those remorselessly incremated hymns will be? (1862, p. 12)

Most of these manuscripts, the article goes on to say, were commonplace or without rhyme or reason. The tone is jocular but the language is strangely violent: The judging committee nominates culprits for extermination. The offending manuscripts will go to a temporary 'tomb' before finally being 'incremated'. How would an entrant on that 'anxious seat' feel after happening upon this report?

The 900 or so entries not accompanied by music were reduced by the judges to about thirty, and second and third examinations reduced that number by half. In behaviour prescient of contemporary *Idol* music contests which make fun of losers, the judges preserved several entries 'on account of their absurdity or grotesqueness. They were so bad as to be good' (1862, p. 12). The judges, insists the article, are 'gentlemen of well-known musical taste and cultivation' (1862, p. 12).

In *Sophie's Choice*, Stingo's despair at receiving manuscripts of 'unrelenting mediocrity', where the coffee stain in the corner is perhaps the most vivid and arresting image, leads to a kind of critical inertia, or at least curbs his ability to perceive commercial potential, or, as he puts it, 'the nexus between good books and filthy lucre' (1992, p. 19). The job was 'a lark' at first, so that Stingo 'honestly enjoyed the bitchery and vengeance' he was 'able to wreak upon these manuscripts', but its sameness becomes enervating (1992, p. 12). Stingo eventually rejects a manuscript that when taken up by another publisher becomes a best-seller and a 'great classic of modern adventure' (1992, p. 19). Stingo recalls his report on the manuscript, noting its 'cocksure, priggish and disastrous cadences':

> so it is of some relief after these bitter months to discover a manuscript containing a prose style that does not cause fever, headache or retching, and as such the work deserves qualified praise. The idea of men adrift on a raft does have a certain appeal. But for the most part this is a long, solemn and tedious Pacific voyage best suited, I would think, to some kind of drastic abridgement in a journal like the National Geographic. Maybe a university press would buy it, it's definitely not for us. (1992, p. 19)

The title he refers to is *Kon-Tiki*. Clearly he was jaded. Or inexperienced. Or simply uninterested in this kind of subject matter and therefore unable to imagine its appeal to others.

In *Sophie's Choice*, Stingo provides excerpts from three other reader's reports, two of which refer to works by women. The first report concludes with the following: 'Utterly aghast even as I write, I can only say that this may be the worst novel ever penned by woman or beast. Decline with all possible speed' (1992, p. 13). The second refers to a humorous memoir called *The Plummer's Wench*, and includes the fact that the author is 'an actual woman, married—as the title coyly indicates—to a plumber living in a suburb of Worcester, Mass.' Stingo claims it borders on the scatological and strives for laughs but is not funny, and further that:

> these illiterate daydreams are an attempt to romanticize what must be a ghastly existence, the author eagerly equating the comic vicissitudes of her daily life with those in the household of a brain surgeon ... This manuscript arrived especially tacky and dogeared, having been

> submitted—according to the author in a letter—to Harper, Simon & Schuster, Knopf, Random House, Morrow, Holt, Messner, William Sloane, Rinehart, and eight others. (1992, pp. 13-14)

Had such an author lived in our time, she could turn to one of many internet sites catering for writers with too much experience of rejection. Many trot out well known success stories, listing writers who were rejected over and over but whose work was then published (sometimes by themselves) only to sell millions or win literary prizes (the two outcomes are not usually synonymous). There are stories galore to appease their fears though the precise number of rejections a work received sometimes changes from site to site. We might learn, for example, how *Harry Potter and the Philospher's Stone,* despite an agent's backing, was rejected by eight publishers before a junior at Bloomsbury encouraged a senior editor to consider it. And famous authors' double-figure rejections are also noted, including: Dr Seuss's first effort, *To think that I saw it on Mulberry Street*, Richard Bach's *Jonathan Livingston Seagull*, Richard Hooker's *Mash*, James Joyce's *Dubliners*, Grace Metalious's *Peyton Place*, Stephen King's *Carrie*, and Margaret Mitchell's *Gone with the Wind. The Diary of a Young Girl* by Anne Frank is claimed to have been turned down by 15 publishers before it was published by Doubleday in 1952 and went on to become one of the best-selling books ever (Oshinsky 2007). The story of an American publisher's rejection of George Orwell's *Animal Farm*, because it was impossible to sell animal stories in the USA, is also gleefully regaled, along with other mind-boggling judgments on manuscripts that subsequently became widely admired books.

Lulu.com goes so far as to offer writers not only a print-on-demand service that enables them to 'reject the idea of rejection' by publishing and selling their own 'book, e-book, calendar ... and now toilet roll, without some lofty editor first having to grant permission', but also a means of disposing of rejection letters by printing them onto toilet paper, so they may put the bad experience behind them (Lulu 2005).

Stories of rejection preceding critical or commercial success are reassuring, and this explains why success stories are repeated and why books about hardship followed by glory, such as three titles published by Pushcart Press in the nineties, are popular. *Rotten Rejections: A Literary Companion* was edited by André Bernard and seems to be the source of many internet accounts. *Rotten Reviews* and *Rotten Reviews II* were edited by Bill Henderson and made it to the best seller lists. In 1998, the three volumes were published together as *Pushcart's Complete Rotten Reviews and Rejections: A History of Insult, A Solace to Writers* (Pushcart's 1997).

Despite the intensity of Stingo's loathing and condescension, and the interest generated by failure, writers' fragile hopes and disappointments can seem rather inconsequential—after all, people aren't forced to write and submit their work to publishers or competitions. However, reaching the conclusion to Stingo's report on the memoir, we are reminded how painful it can be when after a long labour one's baby is stillborn. Stingo writes:

> the author mentions her desperation over this MS—around which her entire life now revolves—and (I'm not kidding) adds a veiled threat of suicide. I should hate to be responsible for anyone's death but it is absolutely imperative that this book never be published. *Decline! (Why do I have to keep reading such shit?)* (1992, p. 14)

Notably, Stingo's contempt doesn't subside despite the writer's despair. Notions of writing being one's baby and of stillborn creative efforts are clichés which suggest the potential magnitude of writerly loss, but the problem evokes little sympathy from Stingo, or indeed from the editor of a major US publishing house early last century—which amuses a journalist reporting on the matter for a 1912 *New York Times* article called 'Humour and Pathos from Would-Be Authors: Eccentricities of a Literary Underworld Known Only to Editors' (1912, p. SM10). The article, all about the hubris and delusion of writers, contains funny excerpts from letters that have accompanied submitted manuscripts. The article claims:

> The editor alone knows how wide-spread is the desire for authorship

> among the sons and daughters of men, how many have their messages which are never delivered: how manifold is the number who conceive themselves chosen to instruct, guide, and otherwise benefit the world, and how large is the stillborn death rate among them. (1912, p. SM10)

Stingo's assessment of *The Plumber's Wench* may be accurate, or it may represent a form of blindness attributable to youthful, male arrogance. Styron, creating Stingo as a version of his younger self, may be exercising some irony: after all, in 1947 an editor like Stingo might still dismiss women's life writing, but when *Sophie's Choice* was published thirty years later, following the women's movement, the publishing landscape had clearly changed. Women readers and writers, and ordinary suburban and domestic experiences, came to figure more prominently in novels, memoirs and poetry than at any time in history. This change had long been in the making, of course, but there seems little doubt that, as the twentieth century progressed, women's demand for stories and characters that resonated with their daily experiences could no longer be ignored for commercial reasons. Some of this material will not be 'literary', of course, and would never appeal to one like Stingo, but an assessor's job is to recognise more than their own tastes. Stingo's scorn, though, is perhaps of a type exhibited a long time prior by George Eliot in her 1856 essay titled 'Silly Novels by Lady Novelists', which criticises 'the frothy, the prosy, the pious, or the pedantic' (1856, p. 1). Eliot's essay claims that the standard apology for women becoming writers is that society gives them no other 'spheres of occupation'. Her riposte is that society is blamed for the manufacture of many things, 'from bad pickles to bad poetry' but that silly writing by women is not the result of labour at all, but of 'busy idleness' (1856, p. 20). What is frivolous to one woman may not be to another, of course. Manguel makes this point when discussing literature by Heian women a millennium ago, who produced 'some of the most important works in Japanese literature', and perhaps of all time (1997, p. 231). The most famous examples are *The Tale of the Genji* by Lady Murasaki, which may be 'the world's first real novel, probably begun in 1001 and finished not before 1010' and *The Pillow Book of Sei Shonagon*, which he tells us was composed around the same time (1997, p. 231). Apparently Lady Murasaki thought Shonagon's book frivolous, but this seems to have been because it closely documented women's everyday lives: 'Shonagon's intimate, seemingly banal style of literature flourished among the women readers of her time', Manguel explains (1997, p. 231). 'In these texts, their readers found their own lives lived or unlived, idealized or fantasized, or chronicled with documentary prolixity and faithfulness ... In Sei Shonagon, as well as in Lady Murasaki, lie the shadows of the women's literature we read today' (1997, pp. 234–235).

When recalling his rejection of the *Kon-Tiki* manuscript, Stingo openly recognises his mistaken reading of the potential readership, but it is possible that Styron is also suggesting that Stingo's oversights may have been more wide-reaching and that even thirty years later he remains blinkered. Editors' choices obviously affect individual authors, then, but they are also significant because they potentially change the course of literary history.

What manuscript assessor or journal editor has not considered the possibility that they will reject a submission that has latent potential—or worse, potential that every other editor would have perceived immediately? Stingo's experience points to a general problem: one reviewer's, or editor's, or assessor's, or reader's response will not necessarily be the same as another's. Everyone knows this, of course. It makes selection a worrisome process and publishing, to some extent, a game of chance.

Interested in this point after judging the Max Harris Poetry Award with Tom Shapcott, I searched the Internet to see what might be found on the subject of selecting prize-winners in literary competitions. Straightaway up popped comments by judges that winning entries select themselves. Do judges, by this sleight of hand, effectively abrogate responsibility for their choices? This contrasts with other judges' claims to be found in cyberspace, but which I have also read and heard over many years as convenor of an undergraduate prize for poetry and fiction, and also as a committee member of various writers' centres that run literary competitions, which is that writers should not be too down on themselves if they don't win or gain a commendation, for it is likely another judge would have selected different entries, and perhaps even theirs. This may be true; in the Max Harris Award a few poems made one or other judge's longlist but not both, so their chances of making the shortlist from which the winning poems would be selected were greatly reduced.

Judging others encourages us to question our own learning, biases, compromises, and preferences. It seems true to say that different judges will make different selections then; but can this be true at the same time as it is true that entries in some sense select themselves? If so, on what basis are they self-selecting? Presumably they are better poems or stories. But in what ways are they better? What criteria are guiding the selection? Do the poems or stories somehow construct the criteria even as they judge themselves to admirably meet those criteria? Or has the writer's best skill been in reading the judge, in anticipating what will be winsome, thus ensuring reader-writer synchronicity? Shared judging, as for the Max Harris Award, seems fairer, since the judges will bring different knowledge and experience to the task, and may be of different ages, genders, and social backgrounds. They can challenge and question each other's choices, and be asked to defend their own. The drawback is that judges may not agree on a final shortlist or on a winner, and so may need to compromise.

Trying to appease entrants by suggesting other judges might have chosen their work states the obvious, perhaps, but seems less a kindness than another means of deflecting responsibility for the choices we make. Nevertheless, such deflections are seductive since it is inevitable that the majority of entrants will be disappointed by a competition's results.

Tom Payne comments that '[t]here are more rejection letters now than at any time in literary history. There are more manuscripts than ever—most publishers receive at least 100 a week—and more people to reject them. These days authors can expect rejections not only from publishers but also from the agents who themselves must wait for the work they're representing to be rejected' (Payne 2003, p. 1). He muses that given 'so many blows to an author's confidence, it's hard to see how anyone can carry on writing', but also observes that 'myriad error-filled websites' consoling writers with success stories are underlined by the premise that 'writers are beautiful individuals, and that publishers are corporate idiots' (2003, p. 1). This view is not so different from Stingo's, except that once again it needs qualifying: those writers who eventually find publication are beautiful individuals, and the publishers who rejected them are clots. Again, where does that leave other writers, the great number who may never be selected for prizes or publication?

This brings me to a final question: what about editors or publishers deemed clots or idiots not because they rejected work that achieves future success (or which turns out to be the work of an established author that has been typed up and submitted under another name as a test for publishers), but because they publish work in good faith only to find they've been duped?

The late Max Harris, one-time editor of the Australian avant-garde journal *Angry Penguins*, was humiliated by a notorious hoax perpetrated by disgruntled poets Harold Stewart and James McCauley. Harris and the literary modernism he advocated were the men's bête noire, so they devised a series of poems and also a poet—Ern Malley—to expose Harris's views and modernist poetry as absurd. Ern Malley was supposedly an unschooled, working class, secretive surrealist who, tragically, died at 24 from Graves' disease. Stewart and McCauley apparently wrote Malley's entire oeuvre of sixteen poems on a single day, by drawing lines haphazardly from their own unpublished poetry and other available sources. Only by rejecting the poems would Harris show proper literary judgement, in their view. However, Harris was excited and impressed by the poems, and with the support of his co-editors and in an act that ended the journal, he dedicated an entire 1944 issue—*The Darkening Ecliptic*—to Ern Malley's poems and his commentary on them.

When he received the poems from Ern's fictitious sister Mabel in 1943, Max Harris was a 22 year old editor—as was Stingo (and Styron) in 1947 when employed by McGraw-Hill. Harris's exuberance in accepting the work of Ern Malley and publishing it in *Angry Penguins* might reasonably be compared with that of Stingo in rejecting the famous *Kon-Tiki*. Acts of acceptance and rejection involve personal risk for editors and publishers, but publishing presents a much greater risk than rejection, for one's choice is made public and both reputation and finances are at stake. Responsibility cannot be avoided. Rejecting a writer's work remains largely a private matter unless the writer, editor or publisher elects to discuss it.

In 1989, US journalist Jack Anderson published an article on the Ern Malley hoax in the *New York Times* after learning of it during a visit to Australia. He had come across *The Poems of Ern Malley*, a collection published by Allen & Unwin in 1987. He rightly claims that '[t]he very idea of fakery sets critics trembling':

> What if the book they are reading, the score they are hearing or the dance they are watching is not some kind of creative innovation, but a hoax? And should the thought then occur that the hoax may be a deliberate attempt by an artistic malcontent to make both new trends and their critical admirers seem foolish, the trembling may increase a thousandfold. (Anderson 1989, p. 1)

Fakery undermines the authority of literary institutions and their staff—publishers, editors, agents, literary critics, prize committees, and book reviewers—but while it understandably unnerves those whose qualifications and right to choose are put in question, the possibility that those sitting in judgement can and do get it wrong appeases some who feel they are victims of other people's literary judgements and prejudices.

In 1961, the late Tasmanian poet Gwen Harwood made newspaper headlines: 'Tas Housewife in Hoax of the Year' (Atherton 2002, p. 155). Her victim was the late Donald Horne who was then editor of the *Bulletin*, Australia's oldest magazine, the final issue of which was published in January 2008. Harwood, who wrote under a number of names, submitted fourteen sonnets in the name of Walter Lehmann, two of which were later exposed as a hoax. The sonnets, read acrostically, said 'So Long Bulletin' and 'Fuck all Editors'. Harwood considered them 'poetical rubbish' that would 'show up the incompetence' of anyone who published them (cited in Atherton 2002, p. 154). Her reasons for conducting the hoax included her disillusion with the kind of poetry published alongside hers in the *Bulletin*; her sense that a lot of people 'couldn't tell poetry from a bunyip's arse'; and also her belief that male poets were routinely accorded more attention and acceptance than female poets, which was seemingly borne out by the belittling newspaper reference to her as a 'Tas Housewife', and a subsequent *Bulletin* article suggesting Harwood had thought she could keep the acrostics her secret but '[s]uch are the fantasies of lady poets' (2002, p. 155).

The business of assessment and publishing, like writing, is certainly strange and precarious at times. As Cassandra Atherton points out, 'Ern Malley and Walter Lehmann were believed to have made a mockery of editors willing to publish their work, but the hoaxes reveal more than the Australian public's delight in the humiliation of editors' (2002, p. 151). Contemporary evaluations of Harwood's hoax poems, Atherton points out, have been much kinder than were Harwood's own judgements upon them, which tends to dilute her criticism of editors. The poems have been said by critics to show 'musical mellifluousness', to 'fulfil the technical requirements of a sonnet', to be 'full of words poetically evocative of loss and despair', and to include 'a small handful of powerful images, even if they do rather tumble over one another' (2002, p. 155).

Ern Malley's poems have often been republished and in a weird twist he is now probably one of Australia's better known poets. Max

Harris's reputation was once in shreds on account of the hoax and, in its wake, his fortunes slid even further for he was found guilty of publishing indecent material due to some of the poems' sexual allusions and fined five pounds. However, he went on to fulfil his early intellectual and artistic promise—as a poet, columnist, editor, bookseller, and publisher amongst other things, and he also appears to have successfully defended his initial literary judgement. As Atherton notes, 'Opinion has shifted from the prominent belief in the 1940s that the Ern Malley poems were 'nonsense' and that Harris was indeed 'insensible of absurdity and incapable of ordinary discrimination', so that it seems that the hoaxers may have hoaxed themselves (2002, p. 153). It seems that Stewart and McCauley's experimental method produced some worthwhile poetry *despite* their ignoble intentions.

Writers might produce interesting material in spite of themselves, or dull material despite their best efforts, but readers' evaluations may also change over time and within different contexts and according to different criteria. This unpredictability may be comforting to some writers, but it might cause others to throw up their arms in despair! If deliberately bad work can be regarded as important and get published, and then be regarded by many as bad, but later be re-evaluated as good ... what of work that is intended to be good (i.e. their own)? Why will no-one publish it? Why wasn't it commended in the 2007 Max Harris Poetry Award? Why didn't it win? Perhaps next time?

## Note

1 According to Ackroyd (1990), *Household Words* and Dickens's next and similar venture, *All the Year Around*, merged in the issue of 4 June 1859, overlapping by five weeks (1990, p. 850). Dickens owned *All the Year Around* in full, so he now had total control over content and direction. The first issue began with the first instalment of *A Tale of Two Cities*, and serialisation of novels was a permanent feature (1990, pp. 850-851).

## References


Ackroyd, P 1990, *Dickens*, QPD, London.

Anderson, J 1989, 'Critic's Notebook; Ern Malley's Triumph: How a Hoax Became Myth', *The New York Times*, 5 December, viewed 31 January 2008, <http://query.nytimes.com/gst/fullpage.html?res=950DE0D71438F936A35751C1A96F948260>.

Armes, VM 1979, 'An Interview with William Styron', *Contemporary Literature*, vol. 20, no. 1, winter, pp. 1-12, viewed 17 January 2008, JSTOR, <http://links.jstor.org/sici?sici=0010-7484%28197924%2920%3A1%3C1%3AAIWWS%3E2.0.CO%3B2-X>.

Atherton, C 2002, '"Fuck All Editors": The Ern Malley Affair and Gwen Harwood's *Bulletin* Scandal', *Journal of Australian Studies*, vol. 72, pp. 151-62, viewed 4 February 2008, <http://www.api-network.com/main/pdf/scholars/jas72_atherton.pdf>.

Casterton, J 2005, *Creative Writing: A Practical Guide*, 3rd edn, Palgrave, New York.

Eliot, G 1856, 'Silly Novels by Lady Novelists', *Westminster Review*, pp. 442-61, viewed 10 February 2008, <http://library.marist.edu/faculty-web-pages/morreale/sillynovelists.htm>.

Lulu, 2005, 'Jilted authors put rejection letters behind them by printing them onto toilet paper', viewed 31 January 2008, <http://www.lulu.com/static/pr/9_26_05.php>.

Manguel, A 1997, *A History of Reading*, Flamingo, London.

*The Musical World* XL 1862, Boosey & Sons, London, p. 12, viewed 10 February 2008, <http://books.google.com/books?id=4YPAAAAYAAJ&pg=PA12&lpg=PA12&dq=the+new+york+daily+times+1862+united+states+national+hymn&source=web&ots=byX6VVMcpZ&sig=P6Ud6rVCrSj-x7TiuehwcLdKGps#PPA11,M1>.

*New York Times* 1879, 'Women Authors', 5 January 1879, p. 6, viewed 31 January 2008, <http://query.nytimes.com/gst/abstract.html?res=9C05E3DF123EE73BBC4D53DFB7668382669FDE&scp=1&sq=writing+is+an+easy%2C+if+not+fascinating+&st=p>.

*New York Times* 1902, Editorial, 'Rejected Manuscripts', 1 November 1902, p. BR10, viewed 14 January 2008, <http://query.nytimes.com/mem/archive-free/pdf?_r=3&res=9900E2DB1E3DEE32A25752C0A9679D946397D6CF&oref=slogin&oref=slogin&oref=slogin>.

*New York Times* 1912, 'Humour and Pathos from Would-Be Authors: Eccentricities of a Literary Underworld Known Only to Editors', 1 December 1912, p. SM10, viewed 1 February 2008, <http://query.nytimes.com/mem/archive-free/pdf?res=9C03E4D61F3CE633A25752C0A9649D946396D6CF>.

Oshinsky, D 2007, 'No thanks, Mr Nabokov', *The New York Times*, 9 September 2007, viewed 10 February 2008, viewed 15 January 2008, <http://www.nytimes.com/2007/09/09/books/review/Oshinsky-t.html>.

Payne, T 2003, 'However, thank you for your interest', *Weekly Telegraph*, 25 August, p. 1, viewed 31 January 2008, <http://www.telegraph.co.uk/arts/main.jhtml?xml=/arts/2003/08/24/borejection.xml&sSheet=/arts/2003/08/24/bomain.html>.

Pushcart's Complete Rotten Reviews and Rejections 1997, viewed 15 January 2008, <http://www.wwnorton.com/catalog/fall97/Reject.htm>.

Styron, W 1992, *Sophie's Choice*, Picador, London.

Woolfe, S & Grenville, K 1993, *Making Stories: How Ten Australian Novels were Written*, Allen & Unwin, Sydney.

# Thomas Shapcott

## Poetry Competitions and the Judging Process

I have been involved as one of a panel of judges in several recent poetry competitions. The number of entries in these has certainly demonstrated to me at least one thing: poetry may not be widely or profitably published these days, but it is certainly an art that is being practised.

As these competitions have been conducted in different states, though all have been national in outreach, I think it is fair to say that they have given me a pretty fair indication of what, for many writers, constitutes this particular art form. Rhyme has not disappeared as a formal necessity, nor has the concept of a regular beat, or rhythm, though it is also clear that rhyme offers more traps for inexperienced or clumsy players, than rewards. If a person has a 'tinny ear', or is lazy about sound or meaning, the English language certainly has plenty of traps for the ostensible rhymester. Our language is prolific with consonants, and vowels are restricted (or worse, are misheard) so that, today, rhyme is a tightrope, especially if the practitioner is determined to make it a mainstay of their art. Rhyme came relatively late to our language (from France and Italy via the Arabic, at the time of the Troubadours) and though our language is remarkably rich in many things, rhyme is not one of them.

Similarly, rhythm is essentially a subtle vehicle, rewarding and gratifying if used to reinforce the sense or to underline some particular nuance of inflection, but when it is reduced to an artificial pitter-patter or mechanical thump, it can dominate expression and detract from proper communication of sense. Good poets have for centuries known that an underlying rhythmic pattern is reinforced by judicious variation and an ear for the pause that counts. A use of the pause is one of the things that gives poetry its particular focus. Many people have delighted in poetry for its particular concentration, its compression. Much of that sense of compression is derived from the way a poet makes his or her statement take, as it were, a pause so as to highlight particular words or phrase; to make us re-examine language, as well as find new delight in it.

All this is to suggest that poetry competitions still attract plenty of entries in what used to be called 'doggerel'—ineptly rhymed verses in usually regular iambic patterns that would seem to conform to some notion of 'poetry' once (many years ago) taught in schools or kindergarten or at Grandma's knee (though nowadays Grandma is more likely to have been brought up on the Beatles or Bob Dylan). I have tried hard to think of the Ballad Tradition as surviving into the twenty-first century, but too many of the verses entered into competition seem resolutely fixed on some nineteenth century traditions, as if radio and television had never happened. I do not think these are post-modernist examples of collage or bricolage or even pastiche, but rather a sort of illustration of how a once-popular tradition lingers on in, at best, a sort of self-parody (and, at worst, a lazy tribute to what-once-was). The depressing thing about so many of such entries, is that so often they have nothing, really, to say. The best examples of these rhymed-and-rhythmed compositions are undoubtedly those which set out to be funny. These often use the conventions they pay tribute to in order to increase the jocularity, or the point. Good for reciting to friends. Occasionally the more embarrassing examples revert to 'thee' and 'thou'.

Recent poetry competitions, however, give ample evidence that poetry is a living form, with its emphasis on language as something to be coaxed and cuddled into tapping into what is exciting and stimulating, while still listening to speech as living sound or words as tricky messengers. Poetry, then, in the sense that here is both a challenge and a reward. And, for judges, there is reward enough. It is up to the judges, then, to make that finally artificial decision: award a first, second, or third, as if writing poetry were at all similar to horse racing.

But before I get to the agonies of final decision-making, I would like to give some consideration to the more interesting aspects of contemporary practice, here in Australia, that to me seem to emerge from my observations in this process. I should imagine that editors of literary journals and papers would come up with similar observations.

Perhaps the most common theme or issue many poets tackle, with more or less success, is the personal, whether it is love, dismay, grief, solace, or even, sometimes, anger. 'Confessional' poetry is still with us. Poetry as a storehouse of emotional states has always been popular. It is a way of finding expression for feelings that may otherwise be lost, or disregarded, or even unallowed to become vocal, no matter how deeply felt. In this sense, poetry is a potent vehicle. And form can sometimes be just the right way of harnessing it, to push the expression into memorable depth, or height.

When I was just beginning, myself, as a poet, the editor Douglas Stewart (1956) advised me in a personal letter 'to begin with the concrete and immediate; you can then suggest the universal or abstract; whereas if you start with the abstract it is almost impossible to revert to the concrete without the risk of coming a cropper'. Judith Wright, at about the same time, in a lecture I heard in Brisbane, put it this way: 'the transformation of the image into something more, and other, than itself is true poetry' (Wright 1957). One of the pitfalls I certainly encountered in the various poetry competitions I have been one of the judges for, has been the prevalence of abstraction, of generalisation, rather than the 'concrete and immediate', with consequent grandstanding or, worse, a sort of soliciting. It could be said, I think, that generalisations can well be the death of poetry.

The poems that held my attention, then, were almost certainly poems which tackled specific and well-founded themes. Sometimes a poem can seem to exist entirely in its depiction of a moment, observed precisely. Chinese and Japanese poetry are superb at this economy, because there is always some other, implied, 'transformation of the image' implicit. Language is like that.

There are certain fashions in subject matter, as well as expression of emotion, that can be both appealing and also dangerous, or provocative. In Australia, when I was first starting out, Judith Wright (1954) implored us all to face the ominous implications of the Atomic Bomb. Yes; bomb poems proliferated, but often in a very oblique way. And the *Voyager poems* (Stewart 1960) seemed, back then, another area ripe for treatment. Discovery and settlement, our Convict past, all that. And some superb work came out of that tradition, though it has perhaps been pretty much worked to death by now. Still, there always remains the possibility of some poet finding new ways to tackle well-established themes.

In his *Essays on poetry, mainly modern* (Buckley 1957), back fifty or so years, Vincent Buckley deplored the number of birds in Australian poetry. He was taking a swipe at David Campbell, Judith Wright and Douglas Stewart, among others.[1] But he was also, by implication, mourning the relative scarcity of poems with an urban setting. He himself was to publish his important 'Eleven Political Poems' a little while later (Buckley 1966), and the involvement of Australia, going 'all the way with LBJ' in the Vietnam War became a turning point in forcing Australian poets to consider where they were and where we were in the latter part of the twentieth century.

Newer poets certainly still have some challenging contemporary issues, if they wish to be part of their society, as well as self-examiners. There is, of course, one rather chastening proviso: fashionable themes can go out of date quickly. In ten years time 'refugee poems' may not have quite the same urgency they have today. The poet, perhaps, always faces this conflict, with immediacy and with 'universality'.

Certain themes, or subjects, remain universal (perhaps even crows, and many other birds, have not exhausted their potential for invention). With the various entries I read there was plenty of variety, and not a little invention. Perhaps some of the overseas fashions in poetry have, as always, been slow to adapt to Australian conditions (or attitudes) but there was still, in some of the best entries, that capacity to monitor and align the poem so that the reader could be both startled (often the *raison d'etre* of experimentation in verse) and delighted at the resourcefulness of the poet. And the effectiveness of the result.

Repetition and change. These still remain key tools in a poet's bag of tricks. There is a human need that responds to repetition, and poets have, in surprisingly diverse ways, used repetition (of words, of phrases, of whole lines and refrains) as a key instrument in getting across their message, and of echoing the song origins of poetry, if you like.

There is another human need, for change, for variety: sometimes repetition is not the right way to go. The English language is remarkable in its wide choice of words to express similar things. If repetition seems careless, it is usually because the writer has failed to capitalise on this potential variety. You do not have to delve into the more arcane words in your thesaurus to find the right examples where variety counts. Indeed, I find warning bells go off if I sense the writer is using exotic or arcane words where more common ones will do. A poem, despite Pound and Eliot, is not the proper place to exhibit your specialist learning.

We live in a curious society. Sport is officially endorsed as a mark of nationalist pride and achievement. Not all societies have the same preference, and perhaps we lose out by discounting achievements in areas such as music, art and writing. Okay, art is permissible if it attains the equivalence of real estate; and music if it is represented by an icon like Joan Sutherland might even make the grade as an examination question for incoming migrants. But Patrick White, our only Nobel literature prize-winner, is already downgraded and reviled, so what can poets hope for?

The answer is that they can hope to be heard, by someone, somewhere. The English poet who died in World War I, Wilfred Owen, once wrote, in one of his last letters: 'in the end there is only yourself, and myself' (Blunden 1955). To know there could be someone listening out there; that is probably enough. We, of course, must listen, too. And we should be reading. I have been reading the work of a diverse range of Australian poets in this very year. I feel rewarded.

In the final judging process, the ultimate winner is very often selected by that least satisfactory of means: consensus. I have been on many judging panels, here and overseas, where this final 'consensus' simply means that a truly original piece of work is sidelined in favour of one that the majority of judges have the least difficulty with. I am pleased to say that in the case of the Max Harris prize this did not occur. We had no idea who wrote the poems and once we reached an agreed short-list the repeated readings led the judges to the same result. Agreement all round. Would that it were always so.

So, okay, at the end of the process of judging, prizes are handed out. And that is excellent for the winner, who can be assured their poem was the 'best' one entered. But we all know that, in poetry, the final balancing act is fraught with difficulties and contradictions. What I can say, however, is that the experience has confirmed, for me, the sense of an activity of poets here that tells me it is, as I said at the beginning, an art form still very much alive and alert in this country.

## Note

1 'In this kind of verse, the hawk population of Australia is clearly and irritatingly larger than the human.' (Buckley 1957, p. 72)

## References

Blunden, Edmund (ed.) 1955, *The Poems of Wilfred Owen,* Chatto & Windus, London.

Buckley, Vincent 1957, *Essays in Poetry, mainly Australian,* University Press, Melbourne.

Buckley, Vincent 1966, *Arcady and other places,* University Press, Melbourne.

Stewart, Douglas 1956, personal correspondence.

Stewart, Douglas (ed.) 1960, *Voyager Poems,* Jacaranda Press, Brisbane.

Wright, Judith 1957, Lecture, University of Queensland, 1957.

Wright, Judith 1956, *A Book of Australian Verse,* Oxford University Press, London.

Collette Snowden

# What next? Poetry after the awards

Once a poet decides to go public, to expose their artistic or creative work, to offer it for consumption, everything changes. The poet is no longer exploring personal expression, or being emptied of an idea or feeling that cannot be suppressed or denied. The essence of an artistic endeavour in which revelation to others is deliberately sought is the desire for a response and reaction, preferably positive, public and loud; anything but indifference.

For poetry and other written work, the absence of substantial markets (Prater 2002) and low levels of financial support ensure that awards and prizes have a critical role in providing a public response to individual endeavour and creating 'cultural prestige' (English 2005). In a country with a small population, unique cultural identity and literature, such as Australia, prizes and awards have a symbolic value far beyond their monetary worth. From a positive perspective, awards and prizes provide positive reinforcement, encouragement and the development of confidence through public acknowledgement. They also provide poets with a measure of success that gives meaning and value to their work through acknowledgement and critical acclaim.

For both emerging writers and those who have worked for years, winning or even being a finalist in a prestigious competition—like the Max Harris Award—is also an opportunity to take the next step in building or consolidating a reputation as a poet. Even those entering an award for the first time make a substantial leap in self-definition when they muster the courage to send their precious work for scrutiny by judges and strangers.

But promoting poetry is a paradox. The paradox created by poetry being everywhere, but also nowhere. Everywhere, because poetry permeates our culture, especially through promotional media such as advertising, but nowhere, because writing poetry is also regarded as marginal, arcane and eccentric, done for love, and best done for free.

In the mainstream media, poets continue to be depicted by a narrow range of stereotypes from fey academics in shabby jumpers, to drunk and drugged lunatics, occasionally even a combination of both; to loquacious bush poets pursuing the spirit of Australia in rhyming couplets, or sensitive, emotional women wracked by torment about something or someone. We know these 'poet' types but we barely recognise them amongst the poets in our lives, which gives us all the more reason for awards to enable poets and their work to be seen by the public, if only briefly.

Poetry is everywhere because it serves whatever need we have for language to explain, express or expose aspects of the world and human perception (Hollander 1998). There is little doubt that poetry allows people to express emotions at significant times in their lives, especially as a central element in ceremonial occasions such as weddings, funerals and other landmark events. When we look for poetry we find it embedded everywhere. In both our darkest and our finest hours, we turn to poetry, and thus to poets, to express and summarise the substance of our feelings, our achievements, and our responses.

To win a poetry award then is no small achievement, but what next for the winner, the finalists and all the other entrants?

## The spotlight shines briefly

An award is an occasion worth celebrating, but not for long, because it's certain that the moment of recognition for the entrants is short (Neil 2007). By all means we should enjoy the wine and 'nibbles', and the sense of community so important to the occasion, but the next day the life of the poet in Australia begins again. And it is a life with specific characteristics (Brown 2005; Zervos 2005).

For those who enter an award as a tentative first step to releasing and revealing their work publicly, whether they win or lose, the most important action is to reflect on the work itself and to go on. Compare and objectively assess the entered work to the winning work, or the work that was selected for publication. Then proceed. What do to do next? Begin by defining what success as a poet in Australian means and what it looks and feels like. Think about the work required to promote your work in an often indifferent and even hostile environment.

## Defining success

Success and recognition for poets come in different forms, but whatever they are in Australia, any expectations of financial reward are, sadly, unlikely to be realised. Fortunately there are several ways to achieve success (Brennan 2007).

Popularity is perhaps the most sought after, but also most difficult form of success sought by poets. Despite its pervasive presence, the market for poetry is limited and unlikely to lead to rich rewards or mass recognition. Yet, the quest for popularity is just as valid as any other. If not, why publish at all? If chosen, it requires a clear focus on understanding and responding to popular taste.

The primary objective of poets seeking popularity is to please as many people as possible with their writing. In seeking popularity it is essential to write for the audience you want to reach, using their language, reflecting their concerns and values. It is vital to accept that in courting popularity, regardless of critical acclaim or individual assessment of quality, the audience gets to decide what is acceptable and what it will pay for. This is quite a different perspective to the 'I write for myself,' approach often expressed by creative writers.

Best selling British poet, Felix Dennis, argues that eschewing popularity inhibits the appeal of poetry and limits its success, vehemently attacking 'the "closed shop" of the poetry establishment that looks down on his work, and poets whose work is too obscure to have any popular appeal' (Coughlan 2006). His view certainly provides a handy riposte for the criticism his work has received. For example, English poet Simon Armitage, in a review of Dennis's work said, 'Felix's writing shows a wilful, almost bloody-minded ignorance of contemporary writing. However, he does what he does—and that clearly works for a large number of people' (Armitage 2004).

Another path to success as a poet is the attainment of 'professional eminence', which requires the development of a career, usually over a considerable period of time. It is best achieved through commitment to poetry through the established means and involvement in all activities directed at promoting poetry, but most of all by working on and developing a body of work that is unique.

Academic life, as a teacher and advocate for poetry, while also building a body of individual work, also offers a means to achieve success as a poet. Full-time positions for academics or teachers of poetry are limited, with only a handful in the entire country. Independent status as a scholar and/or critic of poetry can also be a path to success. Both of these approaches require a long-term commitment to poetry as well as to education and scholarship. Instead of financial reward, success in academic terms is measured in reputation, publication record and through involvement in the scholarly and literary community. The problem and the danger in this path to success, is that it requires a substantial amount of time and effort devoted to the promotion of other people's writing.

A poet fortunate to have work selected for inclusion in an educational text or adopted as part of a school or university curriculum will achieve a measure of success that may be measured generationally through the enforced exposure to an often disinterested audience. Dead poets seem to benefit most from this form of success. Living poets may supplement the meagre literary income from copyright royalties that such texts provide with school visits and residencies, which themselves require a commitment to engagement with poetry through means other than writing, and again a focus on the work of others.

For poets interested in exploring, disrupting or challenging literary and sometimes social convention, the path of creative radicalism may offer success, which can be best measured by critical reception by the academy or recognition by the literary media. Such a path requires a genuine commitment to a poetic existence at the margins of popularity. It also requires continual engagement with critics and a generally hostile public, which despite being reluctant to support and sustain poetry in any meaningful way, reacts passionately to anyone who challenges traditional poetic forms.

Another path to success for poets comes through working with marginal communities, where poetry has therapeutic and educational purposes, as discussed by Mazza (2003) and multiple authors in the *Journal of Poetry Therapy* (1987-2008), or a broader political purpose. A strong commitment to, and affinity for, the group concerned, as well as to poetry, is essential.

Above all, these paths to success require enthusiasm and dedication to 'poetry' as a literary form and practice, which must be pursued while continuing to write. Whatever form of poetic success is pursued it is necessary to work with specific audiences and communities to find and retain support.

### Invest time

Whatever approach to the poetic life is chosen the task remains the same. Make poetry and its place in your life paramount.

Get your poetry out to an audience by all means available, give it away, create a website, learn to accept rejection and submit it for publication, attend poetry readings, record your poems, publish a book. Expect nothing. But welcome any recognition that results from your activities.

The successful poet, must learn to be a continual advocate, even a salesperson, of his or her work—in order to promote and publicise their work in the media and forums where success is gained and measured. In poetry, this may be the most time consuming and difficult task of all because this additional commitment to external activity necessarily comes at the expense of writing itself.

Self-promotion as a poet requires a considerable investment of time, effort and a focus on building a reputation by association with poetry, as well as through the poetry itself. It requires acceptance of the marginal place of poetry in popular culture and the popular media. The alternative is to continue writing poetry as a private passion and enthusiasm, that is, 'writing for myself.' But this approach too, has its virtues.

Ultimately it is necessary to do what matters. Write well. Say something worth reading.

## References

Armitage, S 2004,'Felix Dennis reviewed by Simon Armitage,' *Times Online*, 9 October 2004, viewed 18 March 2008, <http://entertainment.timesonline.co.uk/tol/arts_and_entertainment/books/article491532.ece>.

Brennan, M 2007, 'Surviving Australian Poetry: The New Lyricism', *Australia—Poetry International Web*, viewed 23 March 2008, <http://australia.poetryinternationalweb.org/piw_cms/cms/cms_module/index.php?obj_id=9031&x=1>.

Brown, P 2005, 'Notes on recent Australian poetry: A talk given at the University of Auckland, 14 September 2005', *Ka mate ka ora: A New Zealand Journal of Poetry and Poetics*, Issue 1, pp. 104–121.

Coughlan, S 2006, 'From parties to poetry,' *BBC News Magazine*, viewed 16 March 2008, <http://news.bbc.co.uk/2/hi/uk_news/magazine/6157936.stm>.

English, JF 2005, *The Economy of Prestige: Prizes, Awards, and the Circulation of Cultural Value*, Harvard University Press, Cambridge, Mass.

Hollander, J 1998, *The Poetry of Everyday Life*, University of Michigan Press, Ann Arbor.

*Journal of Poetry Therapy* 1987–2008, Springer Netherlands, viewed 26 May 2008, <http://springerlink.metapress.com/content/105729>.

Mazza, N 2003, *Poetry Therapy: Theory and Practice*, Brunner-Routledge, New York.

Neil, R 2007, 'Pulping our poetry', *The Australian*, viewed 25 March 2008, <http://www.theaustralian.news.com.au/story/0,20867,22010934-5001986,00.html>.

Prater, D 2002, 'Poetry publishing today' in *Book industries and trade Australia*, Cope B & Mason D (eds.), Common Ground, Urbana, pp. 143–160.

Zervos, K 2005, *Multiple pathways through Australian poetry*, PhD Thesis, Griffith University, School of Arts, Brisbane.

Cameron Fuller

# Collecting the Contemporary: Australian Poetry Anthologies in the 'Noughties'

Poetry anthologies have a distinctive way of contributing to our literary culture. Their role may be seen as complementary to that of magazines, journals and individual poetry volumes, but their scope and function sets them apart. They participate in the literary culture, yet they also operate, to some extent, outside the usual sphere of everyday writing and publishing. Appearing relatively infrequently, they tend to operate from a somewhat distant stance in order to observe and represent particular aspects of a poetry milieu. In this way, anthologies help poetry maintain its status as a significant and enduring literary form.

Through the processes of selection and representation, poetry anthologies serve several functions. In the first instance, they aim to document what the editor(s) consider the most important literature of a particular time and place. Presenting a record of the here-and-now (or the there-and-then), they contribute to knowledge about the poetry of a specific moment and location. Contemporary anthologies identify current (or recent) trends and shifts in writing practices, as seen through the eyes of editors. By collating poems from various sources and compiling them within one book, anthology editors construct textual representations. The resulting collections have the potential to shape our perceptions and understanding, not merely of the poems, but of the greater body of poetry they represent. Anthologies also preserve in print poems that might otherwise have had only a brief public life. They give poems buried in out-of-print volumes, or quietly laid to rest in books of modest distribution and meagre sales, another chance to live. In this sense, they provide a space where disenfranchised poems and disenchanted readers have a chance to meet. While such collections are not thrown together randomly, they may nevertheless be opened at random to the surprise and delight of readers who would not be so inclined to open other types of poetry book.

As a genre, the anthology has many incarnations. Emerging either as a single publication or as part of a series, they range from stapled booklets intended for a small audience to sleek productions designed for an audience of thousands. Whether local, national or international in orientation, narrow or broad in scope, each anthology operates within defined parameters. Some invite submissions; others glean from existing fields of published literature. While quality is the defining element in the selection of poems, other criteria may play a part in shaping an anthology. Some focus on the style and theme of a poem or the time frame in which it is published. Many, however, are oriented towards aspects of the poets' identities, their geographical location, gender or affiliations. Functioning more as collections of poets than collections of poems, such anthologies tend to foreground the work of particular writers, as indicated when featuring several poems by each poet.

A number of institutions, writers' groups and organisations produce poetry anthologies. Secondary and tertiary educational institutions publish collections of creative writing by their students. Writers' groups in urban and rural locations present collections featuring the work of their own poets. The Poets' Union and Adelaide's Friendly Street Poets, to name just two organisations, have anthologies of poems by their members and readers. Events like the Wollongong Poetry Workshop and the Poetry and Poetics Symposium (organised by UniSA) have also led to collections that feature the work of their participants.

Themed anthologies are dedicated to a wide range of purposes. Some celebrate love, honour religion or revel in humour; while others set out to instruct, challenge or inspire readers in the ways of living. There are also anthologies of poems designed to commemorate significant occasions such as weddings and funerals. Perhaps because of their thematic concerns, and an inclination to rely on traditional sources, many of these books do not feature the work of contemporary poets. Ron Pretty's *Poems for all Occasions* (2002), however, is a notable exception.

In the past decade numerous single anthologies have offered national representation of contemporary Australian poetry. As the twentieth century came to an end and the new century beckoned, something of a publishing impetus yielded several anthologies, including *Landbridge* (Kinsella 1999), *Calyx* (Brennan & Minter 2000) and *New Music* (Leonard 2001). Representing Australian poetry, much of which had been written in the 1990s, each of these books has a distinctive flavour and perspective. More recently, *The Road South* (Pretty 2007), *Windchimes* (Rowe & Smith 2006) and *Over There* (Kinsella & Pang 2008) have appeared. The latter two anthologies position Australian within an international context: *Windchimes* focuses on representations of Asian cultures in Australian poetry, and *Over There* presents the work of Australian and Singaporean poets within the one book. This surge of publishing activity indicates that the Australian poetry anthology appears to be in good health. It also suggests it is likely there will be further single anthologies of Australian poetry written during the decade sometimes called the 'noughties'.

Two new and distinct series of annual anthologies have appeared in the past five years: the *Best Australian Poems* (Black Inc.) and the *Best Australian Poetry* (UQP). Despite their similar titles and aims, they contain differences in format and structure. The *Best Australian Poems* includes a larger number of poems while the *Best Australian Poetry* includes commentary by the poets on their poems. Both feature guest editors who compile a collection of the *best* poems by Australian poets in the preceding year. Although the adjective *best* can be contested, its appearance in the titles highlights, with transparency, the subjectivities involved in editing anthologies. The act of anthologising literature is one of imprecision: different editors will always generate different results. This fact, however, does not diminish the integrity of anthologies or the reading experience they offer. Indeed, reading the two 'Best Australian' series together can provide an intriguing comparative perspective where the editors' selections overlap and diverge.

This series format appears to work well for publishers, poets and readers. The publishers are able to package Australian poetry in a marketable fashion; the selected poets receive acclaim; and readers can access quality Australian poetry in an affordable and convenient form. Displayed prominently in bookstores each year, these anthologies offer an opportunity to broaden the audience of Australian poetry. However, there may be a downside. As Peter Rose observes in his introduction to the *Best Australian Poems 2007*, these anthologies 'may license readers to ignore the rest of [Australian poetry]' (2007, p.xii). Their self-contained format offers a convenience, saving readers the effort of finding good poetry. It would be crass for me to suggest that anthologies have become literature's fast-food outlets for time-poor readers, and almost blasphemous to infer that the two 'Best Australian' brands are the *McDonald's* and *Hungry Jacks* of the Australian poetry landscape. But let me be cheerfully opportunistic and take Rose's comment further by saying that his very surname is a useful reminder that the word *anthology* derives from the Greek, meaning 'collection of flowers' (Encarta World English Dictionary 2008). In this context, it is tempting to think of the poems selected for an anthology merely as the pick of the bunch. They may be the pick of the bunch, but they do not exist in isolation as if nothing else matters. On the contrary, they serve as pointers to the whole garden, which the reader is encouraged to visit, and unless this happens, the success of anthologies is only partially fulfilled.

A less widely acknowledged type of anthology emerges from literary competitions. While many competitions publish the winning and commended poems, few present a comprehensive compilation of entries. One competition that has published collections for several years is the Newcastle Poetry Prize. This year, for the first time, the Max Harris Poetry Award has published a collection of poems entered in its competition. This anthology is the first in a series, and it features not only the winning and commended poems, but also some of the other fine entries.

As one of the anthology's selecting editors, I drew on my experience as a poet and reader of contemporary Australian poetry. Along with Ioana Petrescu, I set about compiling a group of poems that would form a varied and vibrant collection. Without favouring a style or theme, we focused on the quality of the poems. From the large number of entries in the competition, we could include only a small proportion in the finite space of this book. Thus, we were forced to make some difficult decisions, and many worthy poems had to be omitted.

My own selection criteria were informal. Apart from seeking poems of the highest quality, I looked for a fresh and invigorated use of language and theme. I sought poems that address aspects of contemporary experience, but also venture beyond the purely descriptive and anecdotal to engage with the complexities of language. I was drawn to poems that contain intellectual and emotional riches; that offer surprises and unexpected turns; that generate a visceral response of the kind Ron Pretty articulates as poetry that 'grabs the reader and will not let them go ... that makes the reader declare "reading these poems was like having my head opened with a can opener"' (2004, p.71). And I looked for poems that achieve a compelling experience through subtle and nuanced explorations of subject matter. In a sense, these types of poems select themselves, refusing to be overlooked, insistent in their demand to be read again.

I sometimes feel that reading an anthology is a little like attending a literary event. There is often an air of celebration and expectancy, particularly when first entering the crowded pages. This anthology presents a colourful gathering of poets from around Australia—some well known and some newer. It brings forth a range of voices to play, in whichever way they will, on the senses, the intellect and the emotions of readers. The poetry is variously exuberant, playful, poignant and earnest. Appearing in sequences, traditional forms and free verse, the poems have much to say about the intricacies of contemporary lived experience. Many of them examine the human condition and its relationship to place, history and the natural world.

Through the vitality of writing in this and other anthologies, Australian poetry can reach a broad audience. No single collection represents all aspects of a nation's literature. Each anthology cuts a particular slice of the loaf and contributes to the overall understanding of what is Australian poetry. Anthologies play an important role in facilitating the exchange between poets and their readers. However, they exist as one of many elements in the nexus of poetry writing, reading and publishing. Peter Rose asserts that 'Anthologisation ... is a reward for poets, but a wide, intelligent readership is a much greater one.' (2007, p. xiii). I agree with Rose's assertion, but I would add that if poetry is to find a wide, intelligent readership, the rewards must not only be for writers, but also for readers. I hope that this Max Harris Poetry Award anthology provides rewarding experiences to both writers and readers.

## References


Brennan, M & Minter, P (eds) 2000, *Calyx: 30 Contemporary Australian Poets*, Paper Bark Press, Sydney.

Kinsella, J (ed.) 1999, *Landbridge: Contemporary Australian Poetry*, Fremantle Arts Centre Press, North Fremantle.

Kinsella, J & Pang, A (eds) 2008, *Over There: Poems from Singapore and Australia*, Ethos Books, Singapore.

Leonard, J (ed.) 2001, *New Music: An Anthology of Contemporary Australian Poetry*, Five Islands Press, Wollongong.

Pretty, R (ed.) 2007, *The Road South: An Anthology of Contemporary Australian Poetry*, Bengal Creations, Kolkata, India.

Pretty, R 2004, 'Finding the Live Ones: A Poetry Publisher's Take on the Question of Quality', *Blue Dog: Australian Poetry*, vol. 3, no. 6, pp. 68-71.

Pretty, R (ed.) 2002, *Poems for all Occasions*, Five Islands Press, Wollongong.

Rose, P 2007, 'Introduction', *Best Australian Poems 2007*, Black Inc., Melbourne, pp. ix–xiii.

Rowe, N & Smith, V (eds) 2006, *Windchimes: Asia in Australian Poetry*, Pandanus Books, Canberra.

# Afterword

The Poetry and Poetics Centre was set up and launched in November 2006. We are celebrating now two years of existence and we hope we will celebrate many more. One of the most rewarding activities of the Centre has been the Max Harris Poetry Award, now in its second year at the University of South Australia.

The Centre's activity is supported by the Division of Education, Arts and Social Sciences and the School of Communication of our university, and our poetry prize now offers $3000 for the best poem submitted each year. The first winner of the Max Harris Poetry Award since the Poetry and Poetics Centre has started to manage the award, is well-known and widely-published Australian poet Jan Owen. Samela Harris, Max Harris's daughter, presented the award to Jan Owen at the 2007 award ceremony.

The collection *Poems in Perspex* contains the winning entries of 2007, as judged by Tom Shapcott and Ffion Murphy, the best poems from the 500 that were submitted that year, selected by Cameron Fuller and I, and also poetics pieces about poetry competitions in Australia. Again, Samela Harris generously offered her time and support by writing an inspiring preface to this book, which is the first collection of what we hope will become a book series.

The Poetry and Poetics Centre proudly offers this book to the community of readers. New and established writers are represented alike and we hope that through its diversity of voices the book will make a useful contribution to the current Australian poetry scene.

Adelaide, 7 October 2008
Dr Ioana Petrescu
Director, Poetry and Poetics Centre
School of Communication
Division of Education, Arts and Social Sciences
University of South Australia

## Biographical Notes

**Jude Aquilina** has published two collections of poetry with Wakefield Press. Her poems have been published in Australia, New Zealand, the US, UK and South Africa. Her poems also appear on Coriole wine bottles. She currently works at the SA Writers' Centre and is a peer assessor for Arts SA.

Born in Melbourne in 1954 to Polish-German parents, **Peter Bakowski's** aim as a poet is to write clear and accessible poems, to use ordinary words to say extraordinary things. His poems have appeared, and continue to appear, in literary magazines worldwide and have been translated into Arabic, Bahasa-Indonesion, Bengali, Chinese, French, German, Italian, Japanese and Polish. Peter has been writer-in-residence at the BR Whiting Library in Rome; the Cite Internationale des Arts in Paris; the University of Macau; the Katherine Susannah Prichard Writers' Centre in Greenmount, Western Australia; the Hobart Writer's Cottage in Battery Point, Tasmania; The Arthur Boyd Estate of 'Bundanon' near Nowra, New South Wales; the Broken Hill Poetry Festival, New South Wales. Peter has given poetry readings and poetry workshops in schools and universities and to U3A and writing groups in Europe, Asia and throughout Australia. Over the past few years he has specialised in giving poetry readings in private houses to groups of eight or more. Anyone interested in hosting a private house reading, anywhere in Australia or overseas, is encouraged to contact Peter via his email address pbakowski@yahoo.com. No matter how many books Peter writes in his lifetime they will all be about what it's like to be a human being.

**Elaine Barker** has had poems published in anthologies, literary magazines and newspapers around Australia. Her first collection, *The Windmill's Song*, was published by Wakefield Press in the *Friendly Street New Poets* series in 2003. She has recently completed a new collection.

**sarah k bell** lives in Melbourne. She dabbles in radio, music journalism and sound art and collects musical instruments she can't play. Sometimes people publish her poems. She hopes this will happen more often in the future.

**David Best** (1945-2007) was born in the north of England in County Durham. He worked as a journalist in the United Kingdom before emigrating to New Zealand in 1966. In 1968 he commenced training for ordination and became an ordained priest in the Anglican Church in 1971. He moved to a parish in Brisbane in 2005 and published a book of poetry in New Zealand in 2005.

**Belinda Broughton** is a mid career visual artist who began concentrating on poetry in 2003 and reading publicly in 2005. She has been published in the last three Friendly Street readers and some journals, but has not submitted widely. She has also had her poems displayed in art exhibitions.

**Gerard Butera** is 38. He is working on his first collection of poetry in a soundproofed room in Melbourne.

**David Campbell** is a Melbourne writer who has won numerous literary awards in recent years for short stories and poetry (both traditional and free verse). He has contributed to three poetry books for children, and in 2007 published an anthology of original Australian bush verse and *Morning Light*, a collection of short stories.

**Gaylene Carbis** is an award-winning performance poet and playwright whose poetry and plays have been performed in Melbourne, Athens, Manila, Ireland, Cornwall, Sydney, Queensland and at the Edinburgh Fringe Festival. She has won awards for and published poetry in Australia and overseas. Gaylene currently lectures at the Australian College of Applied Psychology and has taught English, ESL and Creative Writing programs. Her forthcoming work includes a short film and a play-reading at Chapel Off Chapel.

**Kim Core** is a poet who lives in Cowra. She has self-published seven books of poetry. Her books include *Evolution of a Writer, Deep Thoughts, Amusing Anecdotes and Contentious Issues, Taps, Aeolian Songs, Firefox and Touch*. She is still working on *Thirteen Days . ..And Then Some, poems from England and the Mediterranean.*

**John De Laine** is a PhD candidate in Creative Writing at the University of Adelaide, where his thesis includes the writing of a novel in verse form and a study of the aesthetics of 'ordinariness' as a literary idea. Among his many loves and interests are professional cycling, 1960s cinema, Motown music and astronomy.

**jim dodd** abandoned capitals early in the decade of greed is good, has written intermittently since, living much the same. inspired by various and many, he believes that, eventually, it shall all make sense.

**Robby Drake** has written poetry and prose since primary school. Having studied at the University of Adelaide and Monash University, Robby has been a Drama and English teacher, Counsellor and Social Worker. Brought up in rural South Australia, Robby currently resides in Melbourne with her son, husband and cat.

**Daniel East** graduated with distinction from the University of Wollongong's Creative Writing Degree, and his poetry has been published in *Voiceworks* and The Red Room's *The Salon Anthology: 2006.* He is also one of four members of Australia's only poetry boyband, 'The Bracket Creeps'.

**Carolyn Fisher** lives on the north-west coast of Tasmania having emigrated from the UK sixteen years ago. Her poetry has been widely published in literary journals in Australia and the UK and has also been anthologised. She has been a recipient of grants from the Australia Council and Arts Tasmania and is currently completing a first collection of poetry.

**Cameron Fuller** is a project coordinator for the Poetry and Poetics Centre, and he is also poetry co-editor and treasurer for *Wet Ink Magazine*. His poems have appeared in several publications, including *Best Australian Poems 2006, PoeticA, Social Alternatives, Southerly* and *TEXT*. His first volume, *Low background noise,* was published in *Friendly Street New Poets 11* by Wakefield Press. He is currently working on a PhD in Creative Writing at UniSA.

Born in the French-speaking part of Belgium, **Dominique Hecq** first came over to Australia to write a PhD on *Exile in Australian Fiction*. Since then she has published papers and plays and stories on exile (*The Book of Elsa, Magic, Mythfits, Nosy Blood*) until poetry caught up with her (*Good Grief, The Gaze of Silence, Couchgrass*). Her next collection is due later this year (*Out of Bounds*, re.press).

**Judy Johnson** has published three books of poetry. Her verse novel *Jack*, published by Picador, won the 2007 CJ Dennis, Victorian Premier's Prize.

**Alana Kelsall** was born in Hamilton, Victoria. After completing a degree in languages she lived in Japan for five years. Her collaborative book of poetry, *True North*, won the 2005 FAW award for a group manuscript. She lives in Melbourne with her husband and three children.

**Joan Kerr's** work has been published in Australia, the US and the UK and read on Radio National's *Poetica*. She has won a number of poetry prizes, including the John Shaw Neilson Poetry Prize, the Henry Kendall Poetry Prize and the Woorilla Prize.

**Katerina Kokkinos-Kennedy** is a theatre director, actor trainer and writer. She is the recipient of several awards including the Ewa Czajor Memorial Award (1997), the Ian Potter Travel Award (2001), and a Friends of the VCA Award (2001). Katerina was principal Feature Arts writer for Artshub UK in 2005 and 2006 and is a regular panellist for Arts Victoria. She is currently a Theatre Practice Researcher at Monash University and the Head of the Theatre Company's Panel of the Greenroom Awards.

**Jeri Kroll** is Professor and Program Coordinator of Creative Writing at Flinders University. She has published over twenty books for adults and young people, among them five collections of poems including *The Mother Workshops*, adapted for ABC Radio's *PoeticA* in 2006. *Creative Writing Studies: Practice, Research and Pedagogy*, co-edited with Graeme Harper, came out in 2008.

Irish poet and musician **Jennifer Liston** has lived in Sydney, Townsville and Canberra, and now lives in Adelaide. Ginninderra Press published her first poetry collection, *Exposure*, in 2003. White Wave Press published her second collection *17 poems: one for every year of innocence* in early 2008. Visit www.whitewavepress.com.

**Max Merckenschlager** is a retired teacher, native seedsman and agriculturalist. Many of his poems and songs are about Australian history, including Indigenous culture, and the natural environment.

**Mark Miller's** first book of poems, *Conversing with Stones,* won the Anne Elder Award in 1989 and his second, *This Winter Beach,* was published in 1999. A third volume, *Scanning the Horizon,* is in search of a publisher. Mark lives on the south coast of New South Wales.

**Ed Moreno** is a Mexican-American Australian poet. Born in Manila, he wandered the globe for 30 years before settling in Melbourne. He studies writing at the University of Melbourne. His writing has appeared in the *James White Review*, the *Santa Fe Literary Review*, blithe.com, and *Mini Shots.*

**Ffion Murphy**'s publications include *The Gate of Dreams, Story/telling, Writing Australia,* and *Devotion,* and she was the inaugural editor of the *API Review of Books*. She completed her PhD through the University of Queensland and teaches writing and editing at Edith Cowan University in Western Australia.

**Jan Owen** is a South Australian poet whose sixth book, *Poems 1980–2008* was published by John Leonard Press in April 2008. She has been a writer-in-residence in Italy, Malaysia and France and has received various grants and prizes including the Mary Gilmore Award, the Wesley Michel Wright Poetry Prize and the Gwen Harwood Prize.

**Nicola Scholes** is a Brisbane-based writer, illustrator and actor. She is researching a PhD on Allen Ginsberg's poetry at The University of Queensland. Her poems have appeared in *Beer Swill Romanticism, The Broadkill Review* (USA), *Cordite Poetry Review, dotlit, HECATE, The Mozzie, Social Alternatives* and *SpeedPoets* magazine.

**Thomas Shapcott**, AO, inaugural Professor of Creative Writing at the University of Adelaide (1997–2005), now Professor Emeritus, has published over 50 books nationally and internationally, including poetry, novels and short stories. An original Member of the Literature Board of the Australia Council, he was the Board's Director from 1983 to 1990.

**Ann Shenfield** is an author illustrator. Her book *Scribble Sunset*, will be published by Lothian Children's Books this year. In 2007 she won the Rosemary Dobson poetry award.

**Anna Skeer** is 29 and lives in Cairns, Queensland, with her Blue Heeler, Pherra. There she works with Backpackers. Winner of the Youth Max Harris Poetry Award in 1995, 1997 and commended in 1996—she still wishes she had the creativity of her childhood, growing up in poetry-producing Penola in South Australia.

**Alex Skovron** is the author of four collections of poetry, most recently *The Man and the Map* (2003), and a prose novella, *The Poet* (2005). A volume of prose-poems, *Autographs*, is forthcoming. He was born in Poland, arrived in Australia aged nine, grew up in Sydney, and lives in Melbourne.

**Ian C Smith** lives near Bairnsdale with his wife and four sons. His short fiction has appeared in *Australian Book Review, Island, Meanjin, Overland* and *Westerly*, and his non-fiction in *The Age*. His narrative verse has been published in *The Weekend Australian, Best Australian Poetry, 2004, Malahat Review, Quadrant* and *Southerly*. His books of verse are published by Ginninderra Press.

**Collette Snowden** worked in a variety of media positions before becoming a lecturer and researcher in the School of Communication at UniSA. She is also a poet and once performed at the Sydney Biennale before being gripped by the fear of life as a professional artist and succumbing to cowardice.

**Jessica Szwarcbord** is a poetic-on-occasion, nineteen-year-old from Melbourne. She is currently a second year student, studying for a Bachelor of Law/Arts at university and inherited her love of words from her mother, who introduced her to philosophy, literature and poetry.

**Jenny Toune**: Alternating between the rhythms of tap-dance and the rhythms of poetry, Jenny sometimes finds herself craving silence. When not writing or running 'tap jams', she is encouraging kids in the art of dance.

**Amelia Walker** has published one collection, *Fat Streets and Lots of Squares*, and edited for *dB* and *Friendly Street*. She recently featured at the 2008 World Poetry Festival (Kolkata). She also runs workshops. Last year she assisted students from Collingwood Alternative School to write and publish a verse-novella with a positive mental health message, thanks to funding from the SFYS.

**John Watson**: Author of *A First Reader* (Five Islands Press 2004) and *Montale: A Biographical Anthology* (Puncher and Wattmann 2006) and *Erasure Traces* (Puncher and Wattmann 2008), all of which the author recommends without reservations.

**Les Wicks** has toured widely and seen publication across eleven countries in seven languages. He runs Meuse Press, which focuses on poetry outreach projects. His seventh most recent book of poetry is *Stories of the Feet* (Five Islands Press 2004).

Queensland-born **Jena Woodhouse** has published two poetry collections, *Eros in Landscape* (Jacaranda) and *Passenger on a Ferry* (UQP), and is completing a third, *The Book of Lost Addresses*, which includes the poem published here. Her work has appeared widely at home and also abroad, and has received awards locally. She reviews and translates poetry (from Greek and Russian) and is currently completing a PhD in Creative Writing at QUT.

# Editors

**Ioana Petrescu**, Senior Lecturer in Professional and Creative Writing at UniSA and Director of the Poetry and Poetics Centre, came to Australia from Romania in 1996. Since then she has published two collections of poetry and more than one hundred poems in literary journals, edited six books and produced a poetry CD.

**Cameron Fuller** is a project coordinator for the Poetry and Poetics Centre, and he is also poetry co-editor and treasurer for *Wet Ink Magazine*. His poems have appeared in several publications, including *Best Australian Poems 2006, PoeticA, Social Alternatives, Southerly* and *TEXT*. His first volume, *Low background noise*, was published in *Friendly Street New Poets 11* by Wakefield Press. He is currently working on a PhD in Creative Writing at UniSA.

**Gillian Ratcliff** completed a Professional Writing degree in 2004 at UniSA and then undertook Honours where she explored the invisible art of editing. In 2005 she was awarded the Cecil Teasdale-Smith (Literary) Award. Gillian is currently teaching part time at UniSA and working as a freelance editor. She has been involved in editing several university publications and was a contributing author to *Fuse or fracture: English as a world lingua franca.*

LYTHRVM

Lythrum Press

www.lythrumpress.com.au